"Preaching is the rudder of the chur[...] material the Holy Spirit uses to transform lives. Every honest pastor [...] become a more powerful and effective communicator and Sunukjian's Biblical Preaching for the Contemporary Church series is one of the most effective tools I know. His coaching and example have had a significant role in shaping how I teach God's word today and I highly recommend his work to you."

—**Chip Ingram,** Senior Pastor, Venture Christian Church;
Teaching Pastor, Living on the Edge

"These model sermons remind us that exposition should be interesting, relevant, and at the same time thoroughly biblical. These messages should not just be read by pastors, but by anyone who wants their soul blessed by the transforming truth of the Scriptures."

—**Erwin W. Lutzer,** Senior Pastor, The Moody Church

"We are living in a day when Bible exposition has fallen on hard times. There are too few models and even fewer practitioners. Sunukjian is one of the best at wedding solid biblical exposition with creative and relevant applications. His artful use of imagination and penetrating questions in connecting the listener to the text is an invaluable guide for faithfully preaching the ever true and practical Word of God."

—**Mark L. Bailey,** President and Professor of Bible Exposition,
Dallas Theological Seminary

"Good preaching is both a science and an art. While it is relatively easy to master the science of exegesis, the final product is wrapped in the far more challenging art of application, illustration, and delivery. I've found that being exposed to communicators who do the art well has been both instructional and inspirational. This book is full of outstanding examples of sermons that excel in both science and art. If it is true that great preaching is not only taught, but caught, then reading through these sermons will be a significant help in upgrading the effectiveness of your preaching!"

—**Joseph M. Stowell,** President, Cornerstone University

"Sunukjian is not only an influential teacher of preachers; he's also an outstanding biblical expositor. In his exceptional new Biblical Preaching for the Contemporary Church series, Sunukjian wears both hats and helps his readers become more effective biblical communicators as he demonstrates excellent examples of contemporary expository preaching. His sermons are filled with fascinating illustrations and timely application while also reflecting powerful insights into the biblical text. These are books that will encourage any reader—pastor or layperson—and they deserve a place on any preacher's bookshelf."

—**Michael Duduit**, Executive Editor, *Preaching* magazine;
Dean, College of Christian Studies and the Clamp Divinity School,
Anderson University

"Some things can best be taught; others are better caught than taught. Good preaching requires both, which is why we should all be grateful for the unique combination found in Sunukjian's textbook, *Invitation to Biblical Preaching,* and now his Biblical Preaching for the Contemporary Church series. The instruction and examples provided by this veteran expositor and teacher of expositors are unmatched in their usefulness to preachers everywhere."

—**Duane Litfin**, President Emeritus, Wheaton College

"Much ink has been spilled in recent years on matters homiletical. These works have been mostly theoretical and some exhortative, but hardly any modeling of sermons. Sunukjian has done the church and the pastorate a service with his carefully thought out expository sermons in this series of books. The preacher who has an ear will harken to these examples from the pen of a master preacher and teacher of preachers—well worth the investment of one's time. It will sharpen your skills, spark your creativity, and shape your productions in the pulpit, for the glory of God and the edification of his people."

—**Abraham Kuruvilla,** Professor of Pastoral Ministries,
Dallas Theological Seminary

"The best way to learn how to preach well is to copy the masters. Sunukjian's Biblical Preaching for the Contemporary Church series puts into print a wealth of biblical expositions that are worth imitating. Fulsome, gripping introductions draw the reader into the life issue which the text of Scripture—and therefore the sermon—addresses. Ideas flow logically, just as one would expect from the author of *Invitation to Biblical Preaching,* where Sunukjian demonstrates unparalleled mastery of that skill. The content of each sermon is well-researched but it doesn't sound overly academic. Sermons reflect the preaching portion's contribution to the biblical book being expounded. The oral style is engaging and the illustrations not only clarify ideas, they shed the light of Scripture on us who hear them. These volumes will do preachers who read them a lot of good—so long as they learn from the preacher and resist the temptation to copy his sermons!"

—**Greg R. Scharf,** Professor of Pastoral Theology,
Trinity Evangelical Divinity School

"Nearly everything I learned about sermon preparation and delivery, I learned from my former preaching professor Don Sunukjian. His new series, Biblical Preaching for the Contemporary Church, is a must-read for every preacher and teacher who desires to effectively communicate God's timeless truths."

—**Robert Jeffress,** Pastor, First Baptist Church, Dallas, Texas

"From my first bite into the meaty-yet-accessible volumes of Sunukjian's Biblical Preaching for the Contemporary Church series, I was taught and touched by its blend of solidity in depth with insight in content, bringing together an enriching immediate practicality."

—**Jack Hayford,** Founder and Chancellor, The King's University

BIBLICAL PREACHING
FOR THE **CONTEMPORARY CHURCH**

Invitation to Philippians:
   Building a Great Church through Humility

Invitation to James:
   Persevering through Trials to Win the Crown

Invitation to the Life of Jacob:
   Winning through Losing

Invitation to Galatians
   (forthcoming)

Invitation to Mark
   (forthcoming)

Invitation to Joshua
   (forthcoming)

INVITATION TO JAMES

PERSEVERING THROUGH TRIALS TO WIN THE CROWN

DONALD R. SUNUKJIAN

WEAVER BOOK
COMPANY
WOOSTER, OHIO

Invitation to James: Persevering through Trials to Win the Crown
© 2014 by Donald R. Sunukjian

Published by
Weaver Book Company
1190 Summerset Dr.
Wooster, OH 44691
Visit us at weaverbookcompany.com

Cover design: LUCAS Art & Design
Editorial, design, and production:
{ In a Word } www.inawordbooks.com
/edited by Rick Matt/

Library of Congress Cataloging–in–Publication Data
Sunukjian, Donald Robert.
    [Sermons. Selections]
    Invitation to James : persevering through trials to win the crown /
Donald R. Sunukjian.
        pages cm.—(Biblical preaching for the contemporary church)
    ISBN 978-1-941337-04-2
    Kindle ISBN 978-1-941337-25-7
    ePub ISBN 978-1-941337-26-4
1. Bible. James—Sermons. 2. Bible. James—Commentaries. I. Title.
    BS2785.54.S86 2014
    227'.9107—dc23
                        2014012368
Printed in the United States of America
14 15 16 17 18/ 5 4 3 2 1

To my colleagues in the
Evangelical Homiletics Society:

Thanks for your continual friendship,
encouragement, and mental sharpening

CONTENTS

SERIES PREFACE

Some years ago I wrote a textbook—*Invitation to Biblical Preaching*—which has been translated into several languages and is being used rather widely to develop biblical preachers. This current series of volumes is being published as an *Invitation* to sermons on specific biblical books, individuals, or themes. The purpose of this series is to offer models of the principles presented in the textbook.

A sermon comes alive when it is true to the biblical author's flow of thought, clear in its unfolding, interesting to listen to, and connected to contemporary life. Hopefully that's true of the messages in this book.

These messages were originally preached before a congregation of God's people, and then slightly edited to their present form in order to adjust from the *hearing ear* to the *reading eye*. But I've tried my best to retain their oral flavor—I've wanted them to still sound close to the way we talk. This means there will be incomplete sentences, colloquial and idiomatic language, and other features of the spoken word.

I've also occasionally included some *stage directions,* so that the reader can visualize any props or large physical movements that were part of a message.

May God speak to your heart through his Word.

INTRODUCTION

Persecution of Jewish Christians broke out around A. D. 34, following the death of Stephen, causing many believers to flee for safety to other cities and countries (Acts 8:1–4; 9:1–2). As these Jewish Christians attempted to start life over in new communities, they found themselves facing almost insurmountable obstacles. Their shops and businesses were being boycotted. Their children were being tormented in the schools. Their wives were being cheated and hassled in the markets. The citizens of the towns hated them because they were Jews, and the Jews of the towns hated them because they were Christians. The believers found themselves isolated, menaced, and harassed by a hostile world. They began asking, "Why is this happening to us? Why must there be so many hardships? What is God doing? What are we to think?"

Their former pastor, James, heard about their difficulties and wrote a letter to them. Though he refers to himself simply as "a servant of God and of the Lord Jesus Christ," he was actually a physical brother of Jesus, born to Mary and Joseph a few years after the birth of Jesus (Mark 6:3). Along with his other brothers, James did not believe in Jesus at first (John 7:1–5), but became convinced after the resurrection (1 Cor. 15:5–7) and went on to become an early leader and pastor of the church in Jerusalem (Acts. 15:12–13; 21:17–18). He became known as James the Righteous because of his godliness. His congregation also referred to him affectionately as Old Camel Knees—because he spent so much time praying that he had developed large calluses on his knees.

Many have suggested that James's letter is simply a loose collection of exhortations without any logical connections between the various parts or any overall unity to the book. But this is not the case. We will see, instead, that the entire letter is focused on the trials James's friends are going through.

This unifying focus is apparent from the internal *inclusios* that James uses, and from his repeated use of certain key words.

An *inclusio* is the use of similar language at the beginning and end of a section that includes all the intervening materials in a common topic. This linguistic bracketing is the author's way of indicating that all the intervening material is related to the same theme of the *inclusio* language. James's first use of *inclusio* to focus on the common theme of "perseverance in trials" is in 1:2–4 and 1:12:

> *Consider it pure joy, my brothers and sisters, whenever you face trials of many kinds, because you know that the testing of your faith produces perseverance. Let perseverance finish its work so that you may be mature and complete, not lacking anything.* (1:2–4)

> *Blessed is the one who perseveres under trial because, having stood the test, that person will receive the crown of life that the Lord has promised to those who love him.* (1:12)

The similar language of "persevering under trials" to receive the reward—maturity and completeness, the crown of life—indicates that the verses between 1:4 and 1:12 are also connected to this same theme.

A further *inclusio* occurs at the end of the letter, showing that the entire letter is focused on the theme of persevering under trials in light of the reward:

> *As you know, we count as blessed those who have persevered. You have heard of Job's perseverance and have seen what the Lord finally brought about. The Lord is full of compassion and mercy.* (5:11)

This final *inclusio* means that as we read the intervening chapters between 1:12 and 5:11 we should be thinking of how they connect to the theme of persevering under trials. This will drastically change some of our previous interpretations, as will be seen from the expositions which follow.

In addition to the use of *inclusio* to highlight his continuous theme, James also repeats certain key words to reinforce it. For example: In 1:8, if we "doubt" that God is working good through our trials, we are "double-minded."

In 2:4, if we favor the rich man who can alleviate our trials, we have "discriminated" (literally, "doubted") within ourselves as to who is in control, God or the rich man, thus judging between the two with evil thoughts. In 4:8, if we resist God's working through our trials, we are "double-minded." Using these repeated key words, James threads his theme of trials throughout the letter.

In summary, James's purpose is to tell his friends and us how to act, both as individuals and as a church, when we find ourselves in stressful and difficult situations. His comments unfold along the following lines (summarized in paraphrase):

> Persevere joyfully through trials, for they lead to maturity and the crown of life. (1:1–12)

> If you respond sinfully to a trial, don't blame God, but instead obey what the Word says. (1:13–25)

> To safely get through the trials, you must thus guard your tongue from blaming God, and then determine that you will love others and that you will avoid the world's way of responding to difficulties. (1:26–27)

> Determine that you will love others. (2:1–26)

>> Love impartially, for this will reveal your confidence that God is in control of the trial. (2:1–13)

>> Love tangibly, for this will reveal a living faith that will safely take you through the trial. (2:14–26)

> Determine that you will avoid the world's way of responding to difficulties. (3:1–5:20)

>> Avoid lashing out against other believers whose behavior you think may be adding to your difficulties. (3:1–4:12)

>>> Don't too quickly presume to teach others how to act so as to minimize the group's difficulties, for you will inevitably sin in the process. (3:1–12)

>>> If you have "wisdom" for how other believers should be acting during the trial, make sure it isn't prompted by any personal

agenda, but instead let it emerge through a humble example and a gentle counsel that will bring peace to the group. (3:13–18)

If you find that you are angry with someone in the group, it's probably because they have frustrated your personal agenda, and because you have stopped trusting God. (4:1–6)

Instead of being angry with others, submit to what God is doing in your life, accept that things will be difficult for a while, and don't sit in judgment of others. (4:7–12)

Don't arrogantly assume that by becoming rich you will insulate yourself from difficulties. (4:13–5:6)

You cannot confidently predict the future; God alone controls it. (4:13–17)

Attempts to insulate yourself from difficulties by becoming rich will lead to other sins and bring God's judgment on you. (5:1–6)

Wait patiently wait for the Lord's mercy without grumbling against others or compromising your integrity. (5:7–12)

Talk with God about whatever is happening in your life, and pray for others in your group. (5:13–20)

Essentially, James writes to his former church members, "If you want your trials to produce the maturity and completeness that God intends, guard your tongue tightly from anger against God; love your fellow believers impartially and tangibly, for this will demonstrate your faith that God is in control; and avoid the world's polluting responses to difficulties as you wait patiently for the Lord and minister prayerfully to each other."

1

A TERRIBLE, HORRIBLE, NO GOOD, VERY BAD DAY

James 1:1–4

One of the all-time great children's books is *Alexander and the Terrible, Horrible, No Good, Very Bad Day.** In the book, an 8-year-old tells us how his day has been, and as you can imagine from the title, it was horrible. He says:

> I went to sleep with gum in my mouth and now there's gum in my hair and when I got out of bed this morning I tripped on the skateboard and by mistake I dropped my sweater in the sink while the water was running and I could tell it was going to be a terrible, horrible, no good, very bad day.
>
> At breakfast Anthony found a Corvette Sting Ray car kit in his breakfast cereal box and Nick found a Junior Undercover Agent code ring in his breakfast cereal box, but in my breakfast cereal box all I found was breakfast cereal. . . . I think I'll move to Australia.
>
> In the car pool Mrs. Gibson let Becky have a seat by the window. Audrey and Elliott got seats by the window too. I said I was being scrunched. I said I was being smushed. I said, if I don't get a seat by the window I am going to be carsick. No one even answered.
>
> I could tell it was going to be a terrible, horrible, no good, very bad day.

---

* Judith Viorst, *Alexander and the Terrible, Horrible, No Good, Very Bad Day* (New York: Aladdin Paperbacks, 1972).

And so Alexander's day went—misfortunes, disappointments, scoldings. And it ended like it began:

> There were lima beans for dinner and I hate limas. There was kissing on TV and I hate kissing.
>
> My bath was too hot, I got soap in my eyes, my marble went down the drain, and I had to wear my railroad-train pajamas. I hate my railroad-train pajamas.
>
> When I went to bed Nick took back the pillow he said I could keep and the Mickey Mouse night light burned out and I bit my tongue. The cat wants to sleep with Anthony, not with me.
>
> It has been a terrible, horrible, no good, very bad day.
>
> My mom says some days are like that.

It's not only 8-year-olds who have days like that. Sometimes their parents do too. I remember reading once about a Christian father. The church he attended had arranged for a gifted conference speaker named Joe Bayly to come for a week of meetings. The week of the conference came just one month after this man's wife had given birth to their fourth child. The father realized that it just wouldn't work to take all the kids to the meetings, and he also knew that his wife had been cooped up for the past few weeks. So he lovingly said, "Honey, you go to the meetings and I'll stay home with the kids."

It was his first time alone with all four of them, and their ages were five, four, two, and one month. Here's what he wrote in his journal:

> My 4-year-old wants to know why it is that when Mommy goes out, the kids have to go to bed when it is still light.
>
> I tried to feed them dinner, a real disaster; tomorrow night I will feed them in the backyard; they'll eat off of paper plates; and they'll be dressed only in underwear and shower caps.
>
> The kids always want me to read the alphabet book because they know with that book I can't skip pages.
>
> Never close your eyes when you pray with four kids.

I just made a big mistake: I lifted the lid off the diaper pail. That one act clears sinuses, kills roaches, fleas and ticks, and effectively discourages would-be burglars.

I got angry. I said some things I shouldn't have; my five-year-old wants to know who's Joe Bayly and why do I hate him!

We all have days like that—days when the other checkout line at the grocery store always moves faster; days when no matter how hard you shop for an item, after you buy it, it's always on sale somewhere else cheaper; days when you suddenly realize you forgot to put out the trash as the garbage truck passes your house. But what's worse is when it's not just a day like that, but rather a month like that, or a year like that, or three years like that— when life itself seems heavy and hard, times when:

Your daughter's best friend has dropped her and formed a new group, and she is not included.

The kids at school have made it the "in thing" to get on your case, and make your life miserable.

The day you took the GRE you were sick, and because of your score no graduate school will look at you, and now Plan A for your career is dead, and you don't have a Plan B.

A romance looked like it was going somewhere, but never got off the ground, and then totally fell apart.

Your company's business is declining and there are layoffs and even talk of going out of business, and you don't know what you'll do.

You find yourself saddled with someone else's debt, or you have to raise someone else's child, or you're the one who cares for the elderly parent.

You break a bone that doesn't mend, or develop an illness that doesn't heal; or your body gives out, and you're not ready for it to go.

It's not just a bad day, but a bad life, and you say, "Where did this come from? Why me?"

When these things happen and you ask, "Lord, what are you doing?"—what's the answer? When your heart cries, "Lord, what am I to think? What am I to do?"—what's the answer?

One of the writers of the New Testament wrote to people who were asking those same questions—"What is God doing? What are we to think? What are we to do?"

Fifteen years earlier he had been their pastor, but many of them had fled their city when it became dangerous to be a Christian. One of the members of their church, Stephen, had been executed on trumped-up charges, and the authorities were ready to do the same thing to others. And so they fled for safety's sake.

As they tried to start life over in different cities and other nations, they found themselves facing almost insurmountable obstacles. Their shops were being boycotted. At school, their children were being tormented. In the markets, their wives were being cheated and hassled. The citizens of the towns hated them because they were Jews, and the Jews in the towns hated them because they were Christians. They found themselves isolated, menaced, and harassed by a hostile world. And they began to wonder—"What are we to make of all the difficulties we're having? Why must there be so many hardships? What is God doing? What are we to think?"

When their former pastor heard about it, his heart went out to his friends in distant cities. And he wrote them a letter. He addressed them as the twelve tribes, the true Israel, scattered among the nations. He called himself simply "a servant of God and of the Lord Jesus Christ."

Had he been a name-dropper, he could have reminded them that he was also an actual physical brother of Jesus, born to Mary and Joseph a few years after the birth of Jesus. Though he had early on disparaged Jesus, after the resurrection he was convinced of who Jesus was and became an early leader and pastor of the church in Jerusalem.

He could have pointed that out to them, but he was not a name-dropper or an arrogant man. On the contrary, among his congregation he was known as James the Righteous, a godly man. They also referred to him affectionately as "Old Camel-Knees," because he spent so much time praying that he had developed large calluses on his knees.

His heart went out to his friends in distant cities as they wondered, "What are we to make of all the difficulties we're having? Why must there be so many hardships?" And he opened his letter to them by saying, "Consider it pure joy, my brothers and sisters, whenever you face trials of many kinds, for God is making you what you long to be. See past the trial you are experiencing, my friends, see past it and rejoice, for God is working something very good in your life."

Let's read what he says:

> James, a servant of God and of the Lord Jesus Christ, to the twelve tribes scattered among the nations: Greetings.
> Consider it pure joy, my brothers and sisters, whenever you face trials of many kinds, because you know that the testing of your faith develops perseverance. Let perseverance finish its work so that you may be mature and complete, not lacking anything. (1:1–4)

As we read these words, our first response is, "Who are we kidding? Consider it pure joy? What am I supposed to say: 'I'm so happy, I just learned I have cancer!' 'I'm rejoicing, my boyfriend just dumped me!' 'I'm ecstatic, I'm looking at bankruptcy!' 'My husband is out of work, isn't that hilarious!'" Consider it pure joy? What are we, masochists taking pleasure in pain? Is this some psychological gimmick?

No, this is not a case of "grin and bear it." It's not "put on a happy face" and ignore the problem. It's not "find the silver lining."

What is it then? What does James mean when he tells us to consider it pure joy when we face a trial?

Let's first sort out what kind of trials James is talking about, because some unpleasant things that happen to us are *not* what he has in mind. For example, sometimes our sin or our foolishness creates unpleasant consequences for us. Our wrong actions result in some discipline or unfortunate outcome: cheating and getting expelled from school, catching a sexually transmitted disease, substance abuse, knowingly marrying an unbeliever, or losing a friend because we betrayed a secret he or she trusted us with. These kinds of things bring unpleasant results to our lives. But that's not the kind of trial James is talking about.

James is also not talking about normal hurdles or obstacles that God intends us to work through, temporary difficulties in which he expects us to pray and see his power do great things. These kinds of things are not designed as trials, but as triumphs—a time to see God do good things for us, answering our prayers, moving us ahead.

When James says to consider it pure joy when you face a trial, he's not talking about the results of your foolishness or the normal challenges of life. Instead, the kind of trials he's talking about are those where you didn't do anything to deserve such difficulty, and there isn't anything you can do to stop it. You didn't cause it, and you can't end it: a disease that comes not from sin but from aging; financial failure not because of foolishness but because of economic forces outside your control; enduring the dreary routine of a job that family responsibilities prevent you from leaving; the pain of having alcoholic parents; unfair treatment from teachers.

When this kind of trial hits—something you didn't cause or deserve, and something you can't change—James says, "Consider it pure joy."

Consider it. Count it. Think your way through it.

You won't feel an initial happiness. There isn't anything fun about it. But if you'll stop and consider it, if you'll think your way through it, you'll come to the point where you'll say, "Lord, this is going to be an adventure. It's going to be interesting to see what you're up to with this!" There can be anticipation, James says, an excitement that crowds out grief, a readiness to say, "Let's get on with it!"

"Consider it pure joy, my brothers and sisters, whenever you face trials of many kinds." Why? Because God is making you what you long to be. Through this trial God is making you gentle and kind and stable and peaceful and trusting and loving. Through the trial he is making you wise and encouraging and pure and strong. That's what James means in verses 3–4 when he says:

because you know that the testing of your faith develops perseverance.
Let perseverance finish its work so that you may be mature and complete, not lacking anything.

God's process of making you what you long to be—"mature and complete, not lacking anything"—unfolds in two steps. First, the trial is designed to develop perseverance, stick-to-itiveness, endurance in your faith. Second, this perseverance, or hanging in there, will lead you to complete godliness and maturity. The first step is perseverance—submission to what God has brought, willingness to endure it as long as he intends, and not fighting or rebelling against him. And then, when perseverance has finished its work, when you're steadily enduring for as long as God intends, the results begin to show—maturity, completeness, Christlikeness.

A while ago I had dinner with a young couple whose marriage I had performed some years earlier. They were as sharp and joyful a couple as I've ever known—in love with each other and committed to the Lord. At the time of our dinner, they had two high school daughters, the oldest a senior looking to go to college in the fall, the other in ninth or tenth grade. A couple of years earlier the husband had lost his job, and he had not been able to find work in his field since then. To keep things going, he was delivering pizza, doing some painting—whatever he could do to bring in a little money—all the while still sending out résumés and trying to schedule interviews. His wife was driving 120 miles round-trip every day for her low-paying job—teaching small children how to use computers. Their income that year had been $20,000. They had let go of their home, in which they had no equity. They had moved to a city where they had some relatives, with whom they stayed for a brief period, until they could find an inexpensive apartment. Their girls had switched schools several times.

The day before we had dinner, the husband had had his first real interview in over a year for a potential job in his field, a job that would pay a decent salary and get them back into what most people would consider a normal life. I asked him how the interview went, how he felt about it, what he thought his chances were—the usual kinds of questions—hoping that this would be a wonderful break for them. He answered that he thought it went well, he would be interested in the job, some of his qualifications were exactly what they were looking for, but others he wasn't sure about. He hoped he'd get it, but he didn't know what their next step would be.

At this point in the conversation, he and his wife both began to genuinely say such things as, "We're not really emotionally dependent on getting this job. If we get it, wonderful. But if we don't, we've seen that God can take care of us. We've seen him do it the past couple of years. And we know he'll keep on doing so, if not through this, then through some other way. We won't crash or fall depending on what happens with this job."

Their trial of joblessness and scarceness of money, to the point where they weren't sure whether there would be enough to pay the electric bill and the rent for next month, was a testing of their faith in God—"Can God take care of us? Can he keep our family together? Can we go on with the uncertainty? Can we bear living with relatives, and then in a small apartment, being unable to let our daughters stay in one school for very long, traveling great distances for low-paying jobs, and having no idea how we might be able to pay for college for our children?"

The trial was a testing of their faith, designed to produce endurance and perseverance—holding fast to God as long as he kept them in that situation, counting on his power and faithfulness to provide what they needed when they needed it. And perseverance had finished its work in them. Their lives were peaceful, stable, strong. They were as joyful and relaxed and as in love as they had always been. And across the table from me, their senior daughter had been chatting about school, and about how maybe she was a National Merit Scholar semi-finalist, which meant that she might get some scholarship money from a Christian school she wanted to attend, but if not, she'd go to community college or state school for a couple of years.

Their perseverance under the trial had purified them of anxiety and bitterness and blame. It had purified them of discontent and fear and feelings of inadequacy. They were not fluctuating in their loyalty to each other or to God. They were not vacillating in their trust. They were at peace. Perseverance had finished its work, and the result was exactly what James says at the end of verse 4—they were mature and complete, not lacking anything.

Mature: that means fully grown, fully developed, fully godly—at the end of the process in full strength. *Complete*: that means not lacking anything, having all the parts of godliness in place, with every area of life developed into Christlikeness, and not being deficient in any quality, not lacking in any grace or godly character.

That's a goal to be desired, that's a goal to arrive at: mature and complete, not lacking anything.

How might that come about in your life?

Maybe someone at work is the most difficult person you've ever had to work with—crude, offensive, unattractive, incompetent, whiney, fawning to the boss. Everything in you recoils at being around this person. You didn't do anything to deserve having to work with someone like that, and short of quitting, there's not much you can do to change it.

Consider it pure joy, my friend, for having this trial to face, this person to work with. This testing of your faith is intended, first of all, to bring you to obedient perseverance before God. Will you return good for evil when your workmate is crude or offensive? Will you ask about the hurts and wounds that have made him so difficult to be around? Will you be quick to teach that person some office procedure and stay with him on it to protect him from appearing incompetent?

If you will endure and let perseverance finish its good work in you, you will find emerging within you the loving heart of Christ, and sinners will love to be in your presence just like they loved to be in his. Through the trial God will make you what you long to be—as loving and wise and kind and gentle as his Son.

The sequence is not automatic. The second step doesn't just automatically follow the first. The trial is intended to produce perseverance. But you must decide whether you will let perseverance finish its work, whether you will accept that God is doing something good in you through the trial, and whether you will be willing to endure it as long as he wants. If you're still chafing at the situation, resentful that you have to face it, angry with God for not doing something about it—then you've not yet come to the point of submission and faithful enduring.

Somewhere along the way you have to decide to let perseverance finish its work. Somewhere along the way, there must be a gentle yielding to God, a moment of decision where you say, "Lord, I will let you finish the process. Whatever you're producing in me, I want. Keep me steady. Keep me focused on what you're after. Don't let me take my eyes off your love and good work in me." Let perseverance finish its work, and you will be mature, complete, lacking nothing.

What's the trial right now for you? What's the testing of your faith? Poor health? Loneliness? A hyperactive child? A wall in your career? Overwhelming professional demands? Domestic tedium? Disappointment in a friendship?

The testing of your faith is to develop perseverance with God. If you'll let perseverance finish its work, you'll become mature and complete, not lacking anything in the way of godliness and strength. God is making you what you long to be.

2

KNOWING WHAT'S GOING ON

James 1:5–12

William Shakespeare, in his play *As You Like It,* has a humorous section on the "seven ages of man." He describes how we start out in life and then go through seven stages from beginning to end. His seven stages are: crying infant, unwilling schoolboy, sighing lover, professional soldier, pot-bellied judge, decrepit old codger, and finally, senile oblivion.

These may have been the appropriate seven stages for Shakespeare's day, but today, in our modern Information Age, we need a more up-to-date set of categories. Today, we have a knowledge explosion. Everything revolves around *knowing*—knowing what's happening, knowing what's in and what's out, knowing what's hot and what's not, knowing the lay of the land and how to act. So today, if we wanted to describe the seven ages of man, we would more appropriately follow the various stages of knowing and not knowing.*

The first stage is: *Not knowing what's going on, and not knowing that you don't know.* This would be like Shakespeare's crying infant—living in a bubble of blissful ignorance. With some Americans, this can last until age twenty-three or marriage, whichever comes first.

The second stage is: *Not knowing what's going on, and knowing that you don't know.* This takes place about the time you go to school and notice that the other kids in small groups are laughing at you. You realize you've done something incredibly stupid but you don't know what it was.

---

* What follows is a paraphrase of an article by Donald Kaul: http://articles.philly.com/1992-04-07/news/26001856_1_information-age-modern-man-ideas.

The third stage is: *Not knowing what's going on, but pretending to know.*
This happens when you and your friends share misinformation and laugh at
the new kids who are still back at stage two. You're still as dumb as ever, but
at least you feel superior.

The fourth stage is: *Knowing what's going on.* This stage occurs somewhere in your early to mid-twenties. It's a time when you're perfectly clued
in to all the new trends and fads, when you've seen the hot movies, and
you've read the latest best sellers. You're in perfect sync with your culture.
This stage lasts about fifteen minutes.

Then comes the fifth stage: *Not knowing what's going on, and wishing you
did.* This comes over you in your thirties. One day you notice that you're the
only one at the party with pleated pants or the wrong-length skirt, or that
your tie is too wide or too narrow, or that your makeup is out of date. And
you wonder, "When did life pass me by?"

The sixth stage is: *Not knowing what's going on and not caring.* Most of
middle age is like this—you kind of get used to being "not with it." Finding
out what's up to date isn't quite as important as remembering where you left
your phone.

The final stage is: *Not knowing what's going on and being glad that you
don't.* Not only can you no longer name the top ten tunes, but you've also
never even heard of the people screeching them. You can pick up a super-
market tabloid and you don't know half the people mentioned. It's a wonderful stage. You don't know the difference between Jimmy Fallon and
David Letterman because you've done the sensible thing and gone to bed
before either of them has come on TV.

In terms of pop culture, not knowing what's going on is no big deal.
But in terms of what God may be doing in our lives, not knowing what's
going on can matter a lot. If there's anything we want to know, it's what God
is doing in our lives. Especially when what's going on has some purpose,
some goal.

God often purposely does something in our lives to remove an area of
immaturity or deficiency in us. He sends us certain trials or circumstances
to work on something lacking in us. The trials are designed to make us more

mature, fully complete in godliness, no longer lacking in any area. As James wrote to some former members of his church:

> Consider it pure joy, my brothers and sisters, whenever you face trials of many kinds, because you know that the testing of your faith produces perseverance. Let perseverance finish its work so that you may be mature and complete, not lacking anything. (1:2–4)

But this raises the question, "What is it in me that's immature or incomplete that God needs to work on? What am I lacking that he has to send a trial to address?" And we have this feeling of not knowing what's going on. So we wonder:

> God, my spouse and I aren't getting along, or my child is acting up, or my parents are being difficult, or I'm having problems with my boss. Can you tell me what's going on? Does this mean there's something in me that you're trying to get at and change? If so, what?
>
> God, I have allergies that won't go away, or I'm stuck in a job I don't like, or my car needs repair every month. You tell me to consider it pure joy when I face a trial, because you're using the trial to make me what I long to be. But God, I don't see what you're getting at. What area are you trying to get at it through this trial? What's going on, what are you after?
>
> God, I can't figure out my career, or I can't get the classes I want, or I'm no closer to marriage than I was a year ago. You want me to persevere, but Lord, it would be easier for me to do that if I knew what you were after in me through this. Lord, what's going on, what are you doing?

If that's your question—"What's going on?"—then God is absolutely ready to give you an answer. If you want to know what area of godliness he's forming in you through the trial, he's ready to tell you. He's an openhanded God. According to James, that information is readily available.

> If any of you lacks wisdom, you should ask God, who gives generously to all without finding fault, and it will be given to you. (1:5)

"If any of you lacks wisdom, you should ask God, . . . and it will be given to you." This is not a promise for students taking exams. I heard a group of college students who got together outside a classroom door before a major test, and one of them prayed, "Lord, help those of us who studied to remember what we studied, and help those of us who didn't study to remember what we learned in high school."

"If any of you lacks wisdom . . ." This is not a promise for students. Nor is it even a promise for wisdom in general. "Lord, is it too soon for my daughter to get her ears pierced? Lord, should I take my money out of mutual funds and put it into Treasury Bills?" These may be good things to pray about, and God may give you some guidance. But that's not what James is talking about here.

Instead, this is a promise for wisdom about why your trial is occurring. If you don't know what God is doing in your life, ask him. If you lack wisdom as to what area of your life he's trying to make more Christlike, ask him.

God will be very openhanded with the answer. He'll quickly and completely tell you what he's doing, generously giving you the information you want. The word *generously* has two nuances, two shades of meaning. It's a word that looks at both the amount and the attitude of God's giving; at both *how much* he'll tell you and *how happy* he is to do it.

First, it looks at the amount of information God will give you, how much he'll tell you about what he's doing in your life. He'll reveal to you completely what he's after—what specific area of maturity he's working on through the trial. When you ask for wisdom or insight into what's happening, he'll fully, liberally, and generously give you the answer. That's the amount, how much he'll tell you.

But the word *generously* also looks at the attitude of God's giving, how happy he is to let you in on what he's doing. He'll gladly give you the information, and he'll give it freely, quickly, and without hesitation. He's delighted to do it. It's there just for the asking. That's the attitude of God's giving.

Perhaps the best word we have to convey these two nuances is "openhanded." That seems to carry both shades of meaning: "Take all you want, and I'm glad to give it to you."

When my children used to ask me for something, I wasn't exactly like that. I usually made them justify why they needed so much. And though I usually ended up giving it to them, I wasn't exactly delighted to do it. They had to pry it out of me; I often was a reluctant giver.

Further, I sometimes made them feel bad while they were asking, like they shouldn't be asking in the first place: "Why do you need this? Don't you have enough money for it already? What did you do with the money you had from . . ." I made it kind of unpleasant for them to ask.

But God's not like that. James says that God not only gives generously, openhandedly, but he also gives without making you feel bad in the process—he doesn't find fault. Look again at verse 5:

> If any of you lacks wisdom, you should ask God, who gives generously to all without finding fault, and it will be given to you.

Without finding fault—that means without making you feel bad that there's some immaturity or lack that still needs addressing. When you say, "God, I'm hurting in this trial, and I know there's some area of my life that you're maturing, and I want to know what it is so I can hang in there," God doesn't find fault. He doesn't say back, "Okay, here's the problem. And frankly, I'm disappointed that we still have to deal with it. It's a shame we still have to work on it. You ought to have taken care of it by now. We went through this three years ago, and you made some progress, but you've slipped back. You've asked me, so I'll tell you what I'm doing, but it's too bad that it's even necessary for us to keep working on this."

No, God never finds fault. Instead he answers back, "Here's the wisdom you've asked for. And don't be discouraged. I'm doing something very good in your life. This will make you more like my Son when it's over."

When you say, "God, I'm sorry it's still there," he says, "But isn't it wonderful that I'm removing it?"

Ask God for wisdom about the trial. He'll give it openhandedly, without finding fault.

How does that work? How does God give us the wisdom we've asked for? How does he reveal what the trial is accomplishing?

The wisdom could come to us in several different ways. It might come through the words of a family member or a friend, who might say something like, "You always . . ." or "I wish you wouldn't . . ." These words could be spoken in anger or frustration; they could be said strongly or tentatively, but through these words you hear God speaking to your heart: "This is what I'm working on."

Another way God's wisdom might come is while you're reading the Bible, and something on the page makes you stop, and you begin to think deeply about how the words fit your situation. That happened to me several years ago when I was pastoring in Austin, Texas. I was angry and resentful over the former youth pastor. He had left our church to go pastor a church just a few miles from us, and our whole college department, and about 20–30 percent of the rest of our congregation had gone with him. As a result of all those people leaving, we were hurting—we were discouraged, we lost a lot of teachers, we were struggling financially. And I was angry and upset with him. My whole spirit was screaming "Aaarrgghh!" against him, and I wanted God to take him down, to pay him back in some way for what he'd done to us.

And then one day I was reading these verses in James:

What causes fights and quarrels among you? Don't they come from your desires that battle within you? You desire but do not have, so you kill. You covet but you cannot get what you want, so you quarrel and fight. (4:1–2a)

And God said, "That's why you're upset with him—because you want something, and he's keeping you from having it, so you're out of sorts with him. You want something, you covet something—you want a big church, you want a thriving ministry, you want a reputation as the most successful pastor in town. You've got all this pride and ambition and ego inside you, and he's stopping all those things from happening, so you want to see him taken down. You wonder why all this is happening to you? Don, I love you, and you're doing a good work for me, but we need to address this crud that is still in your heart—this pride and ambition and ego. And that's what I'm working on in you."

Sometimes the wisdom comes from what someone else may say to you, or from something you read in the Bible. Another very likely way that the wisdom may come is that you'll be praying about the trial, agonizing over it, asking God to remove it, change it, take it away, make it different. And then in the middle of your praying your mind will start thinking about the trial. You'll start thinking about the person, or the situation, and something will occur to you, and you'll start pondering that. Some insight will come to you, you'll think of something you need to say, something you need to do.

In the middle of your prayer it will seem like your mind has started wandering down some path. Pretty soon you shake your head, rebuke yourself, and say to the Lord, "Lord, I'm sorry. I got off-track in my praying. I wish my mind didn't wander so much when I'm praying." But your mind wasn't wandering. That was God speaking back to you. You were praying, asking for wisdom, and he started speaking back to you through your own thoughts. You thought your mind was wandering, but in reality, God was working through your thoughts to bring his wisdom to you.

Do you want to know what God is doing in your life through your trial? Ask him. He'll gladly give you the answer. And he won't make you feel bad that there's something he's working on. He'll open his hands to you with wonderful kindness. That's the promise of Scripture.

But in order for this promise to take place, there is one condition. There's one requirement when you come and ask for wisdom. You must come with a trusting, believing heart. You must come convinced that whatever is happening, God is being good to you, and you must not doubt at all that he is working good in your life. You must come with a gentle, yielded spirit.

That's what James goes on to say—you must come with a trusting, believing heart:

> But when you ask, you must believe and not doubt, because the one who doubts is like a wave of the sea, blown and tossed by the wind. That person should not expect to receive anything from the Lord. Such a person is double-minded and unstable in all they do. (1:6–8)

When you ask, you must believe that God is working good in you through the trial. You must not doubt that he's brought it to you in order to make you mature and complete. You must have the kind of faith that says, "Lord, I want to know so that I can persevere, so that this trial can finish its good work in me."

If we want God's wisdom, we can't come with the attitude that says, "Lord, why is this here? Huh? Huh? Why? Why is it here? How long is it going to last? When can we get rid of it?" That's quarrelsome, argumentative, rebellious, defiant. If we come with that spirit, we're obviously in no mood to have God put his finger on something lacking in us. Just as an angry or rebellious child doesn't want to hear anything a parent is saying, so we're in no mood to hear God's answer unless we come with the belief that he's a loving and good God.

If you doubt that God is doing something good through the trial, you'll not get an answer or a sense of direction. You'll never find out what is happening so that you can cooperate with it. Instead, you'll lash out in all directions. You'll be like a wave of the sea—tossed first this way, then that. Notice again verses 6–8:

> But when you ask, you must believe and not doubt, because the one who doubts is like a wave of the sea, blown and tossed by the wind. That person should not expect to receive anything from the Lord. Such a person is double-minded and unstable in all they do.

If you doubt that God is being good, you'll be like a cork in a turbulent sea. It disappears into a trough; it swells to the top. The tide moves it one way, the wind whips it another way. Back and forth, up and down, this way and that.

Double-minded: that means you're unable to decide whether the trial is God working on something in you, or just the result of other stupid people in your life who need to be taught a thing or two and told where to get off. Settle in your mind that God is working good in your life, that he's in control of what's happening and that his goal is to bring you to maturity and completeness. Don't ever doubt that God is good. Come with a trusting, believing heart, willing to hear his wisdom and to persevere with him until his good work is accomplished.

Finally, James gives a couple of quick examples of the kind of wisdom God will give in a trial. The first example is of someone who's gone a long time without having enough money, someone whose finances have been unbelievably tight for months and years on end and who never seems to get caught up or get ahead. This person asks for wisdom: "Lord, why? I work hard, but one thing or another comes up. I believe you're doing something. For some reason you've kept us on a thin edge economically for a long time. Do you see something that still needs to form in us? I'm asking for wisdom, trusting your goodness."

And the answer comes back, "My child, I want you to be more impressed with the eternal riches that I've given you. I want the high position that I've given you for eternity to fill your thoughts more. I want you to take pride in that and to see what a great honor I've given you."

Believers in humble circumstances ought to take pride in their high position. (1:9)

That's the first example—going without money for a long time. What God may be working on is a greater wonder and joy over our eternal riches.

Then James gives us his second example—someone who's lost a lot of money in the last few years. Income has dropped, property values have fallen, investments have turned sour, retirement is shaky. And he asks: "God, everywhere I look, my finances are unraveling. Is there something you're addressing in me through this? I trust your goodness. What wisdom can you give me?"

And the answer comes back, "I want you to realize more deeply that it's what you do for eternity that matters, that your life is not caught up in your business, your career, your home, your car, your clothes, your vacations. All these things disappear. They all perish. None of them really matters all that much. What really matters is, 'What are you doing for me that will last for eternity?'"

That's the second example—losing a lot of money in a short period of time. What God may be working on is a greater realization that ultimately all these things don't matter near as much as preparing for eternity.

But the rich should take pride in their humiliation—since they will pass away like a wild flower. For the sun rises with scorching heat and withers the plant; its blossom falls and its beauty is destroyed. In the same way, the rich will fade away even while they go about their business. (1:10–11)

Consider it pure joy whenever you're facing a trial. God is making you what you long to be. He's bringing you to maturity and completeness. You're beginning to look like his Son. Let God finish his good work in you, and you'll have a life that is full and strong and filled with delight. That's James's conclusion in verse 12:

Blessed is the man who perseveres under trial because, having stood the test, that person will receive the crown of life that the Lord has promised to those who love him.

"That person will receive the crown of life." That's not eternal life. We don't get eternal life by persevering in a trial. We get eternal life by faith in Christ as our Savior. The crown of life is what you receive as you move through the experiences of life. In the New Testament world, the crown was a garland of leaves that was placed on the victor's head, a circle of flowers on the head of the wedding couple, a lacework of gold that the king wore in his coronation parade. The crown meant that you were the center of admiring attention, that you were full of joy, and that everyone around you acknowledged that great fortune had come to your life.

The crown of life, my friend! That's what God is promising, if you let him finish his good work in you.

3

KEEPING THE TRIAL FROM BECOMING A TEMPTATION

James 1:13–21

Let's suppose that you work for a large company. You like your job, but you're not getting ahead—your skills, your abilities, are not being recognized. You need some way to stand out, some way to call attention to yourself, some way to get noticed by the higher-ups so that your career can advance. But at the moment, there's nothing about the projects you're working on or the assignments and responsibilities you have that is going to make that happen. There's nothing in anything you're doing that would cause senior management to take sudden notice of you and mark you out for advancement.

You and your coworkers often go to lunch together. Of course, you talk about the company. Occasionally people in the group have a good idea for how the company ought to do things, or what they would do if they had more influence in the company. During one of these lunches, one of your coworkers came up with a really great idea—an idea that would increase the company's profit margin on a particular product, or that would streamline some process in the company and cut down on overhead, or that would bring the company a lot of good publicity in the media. It was really a good idea. Everybody at lunch said to the person, "What a great idea! You ought to take it to one of the higher-ups in the company." Your coworker agreed to give it some thought, and would probably write up a proposal and submit it.

A few days later, you're representing your company at some convention or seminar, and you discover that your company's vice president is one of the presenters at the event. During one of the lunch breaks, you see him in the buffet line in the hotel ballroom, and you manage to get into the line right next to him. You introduce yourself, and he invites you to sit at the same table with him during lunch. This is great—maybe this is your chance to become more than just a name to one of the higher-ups.

As you're chatting at lunch, the vice president happens to mention that the company leaders aren't particularly happy with the profit margin on a particular product, or are considering how a certain process could somehow be streamlined for greater efficiency and less overhead, or are concerned about some negative publicity they've gotten in the press lately, and they were wondering what they could do to counteract that. And when he mentions one of these things, you suddenly remember your coworker's idea. You realize that it's the exact answer for what the vice president is talking about. It's the perfect idea for what the company is trying to make happen—increased profits, or streamlined efficiency, or media publicity. And you think to yourself, "This is my chance to impress the vice president. I'll tell him the idea. He'll see immediately how good it is, and be terribly impressed with me. It'll give him the impression that I'm constantly thinking about the company, that I have good ideas, and he'll probably remember me. This is the shot in the arm that my career needs. It's not really my idea—it's my coworker's—but the vice president won't know that. What a great opportunity to finally get ahead in the company."

But before you say anything to the vice president, an internal thought causes you to pause: "Should I take credit for someone else's idea? Should I give him the impression that it's *my* idea—that I thought it up? That's not really honest. And yet, I need something to get my career off the dime."

And then you begin to wonder, "Is this a test? Is God testing me? Is God testing me to see whether I'll sin by taking credit for someone else's idea?"

Let's imagine another situation. Your days are incredibly busy. Maybe you're a student. You have classes all morning—hard classes, heavy workloads, tough teachers. You eat lunch in the car while you drive to your part-time job in the afternoon. Then you head home for supper somewhere around six-thirty or seven o'clock in the evening. You try not to eat too heavy because you've got five hours of homework ahead of you. Around eight o'clock, you finally settle down for the five hours of homework. You turn on the family computer to do some more work on the term paper you've been writing for one of your classes, but you can't find it in the computer. And you realize, "Someone else was using the computer and erased my paper or deleted that file! It's gone. All my work—gone! Weeks of work—gone! Who did this?"

Or maybe you're a young mom, home with small children all day. One of them has been sick—throwing up in bed or on the floor—which means extra scrubbing, doubling the load of laundry. Because of all the extra cuddling of the sick child, you haven't been keeping close tabs on the others. And because they haven't been supervised, they've dug up your small flowers in the backyard, or they've written with markers on the wall in the hallway, or they've let the dog in the house, and the dog has knocked over a vase and broken it, or jumped on the couch and emptied his bowels. Another mess to clean up, and while you're getting rags and soap, the two-year old is screaming to get up off the potty-training toilet. And you think to yourself, "I can't take it anymore!"

Or maybe you're a dad of school-aged children. Things are piling up at work. You've been going in early, sometimes coming home late. You try to get home before the kids have to go to bed. Sometimes you even make it in time to help them a bit with their homework. On Saturdays, you're coaching one of their soccer teams, or taking the kids to gymnastics class, and trying to keep the yard in shape. You're incredibly busy; life is a blur. One Sunday after church you're packing your suitcase to catch a plane to Dallas for two days of meetings with a client. You're looking for the new shirts and the one good suit that your wife took to the cleaners on Wednesday and was supposed to pick up Friday or Saturday. "Honey, I can't find the suit and shirts I need to take with me to Dallas? Where are they?" Silence. "Honey!?" "I forgot to pick them up." "What? No! Nooo!"

You're overwhelmed, on edge with all the demands—school, kids, work. You have no spare time in your days, no margins in your life. And then comes an erased computer file, or a house in turmoil, or having to leave on a sales trip when not looking your best. You harbor pent-up frustration, you're ready to explode, you're gearing up for a search-and-destroy mission on somebody else in the family.

Is God testing you to see whether you'll blow up? Is God increasing the pressure to see whether you'll crack? Is God tempting you, to see whether you'll sin?

James has written that we should consider it pure joy when we find ourselves facing difficult trials in life, because God is working through these trials to make us what we long to be—spiritually mature, complete in every area of godliness, not lacking anything. If we have questions about what God is working on in us, if we lack wisdom as to what he's doing, we can ask him, and he'll tell us. He'll be very openhanded about it. And if we persevere, if we hang in there and trust him with the process, the result will be a life crowned with joy and strength and absolute delight.

But suppose, instead of persevering, we get weary of the trial. Suppose we get tired of how long it's been going on. We get frustrated. We're ready for it to be over. And in our frustration, we finally end up doing something wrong. We sin.

We're frustrated with a career that's going nowhere, and so we steal someone else's idea and pass it off as our own.

We're tired of jam-packed days, relentless busyness, no time to take a deep breath, and everybody wanting a piece of us. And then comes some straw that breaks the camel's back, and we explode, we blow up, we take out our frustration by screaming at someone else.

Or, we're single and we want to be married. We're trying to keep our purity, but it's hard. Most other people our age are having sex—they're married, or they're living together, or they're sleeping around—but one way or another they're having sex and we're not. God hasn't brought anyone to us, and nothing's on the horizon. But then we go on a date, maybe a couple of dates, and we start getting signals that the other person might be ready to go all the way. And we find ourselves thinking, "Why shouldn't I? Everyone else would. I'm tired of waiting. I've gone long enough without it."

Is God testing us, stringing us out to see how long we go before we break—before we steal an idea, or blow up in anger, or quit on our purity?

Is God testing us through the trial to see how long we'll go before we give up or give in? Is God tempting us, to see whether we'll sin or not?

James is very quick to tell us that the temptation is not from God. God is not tempting you to see whether you'll sin.

> *When tempted, no one should say, "God is tempting me." For God cannot be tempted by evil, nor does he tempt anyone.* (1:13)

God himself is never tempted to do evil, and he never tempts anyone else to do evil. God never has anything to do with evil in any way at all. He himself never struggles with evil, and he would never cause anyone else to struggle with it. He's never enticed by it, and he would never put it in front of others to see whether they'd do it. Wherever that temptation's coming from, it's not coming from God.

So where is it coming from? What is the source of the temptation? James says it's coming from somewhere inside us. Some self-centered desire within us is causing the temptation. Something we want very much for ourselves rises to the surface, and then an evil way to get it pops into our mind. And if we don't deal immediately with the evil thought, it gets a firmer grip on us and we find ourselves moving in the direction of sin. The evil thought takes over and grows, and becomes more powerful and compelling until we finally act on it, and the result is sin and devastation.

The temptation comes from some self-centered desire in us that entices us and takes over, and the results are disastrous:

> *But each person is tempted when they are dragged away by their own evil desire and enticed. Then, after desire has conceived, it gives birth to sin; and sin, when it is full-grown, gives birth to death.* (1:14–15)

We're tempted by something we want, some self-centered desire in us. We're dragged away and enticed by it. *Dragged away*: like a fishhook is caught in our mouth and is pulling us. *Enticed*: like an animal seeing a tidbit that it wants, not realizing it is bait in a trap that will close on him.

Some self-centered desire entices us. Such as:

"My career's going nowhere. I want more recognition, more money, more influence. I want to be more at the center of things. I want to be one of the decision-makers. I want to be in the inner circle." Impatience. Ambition. A self-centered desire.

"I'm an overloaded student, or mom, or dad. It would be nice to get a little more credit for how hard I'm working. People ought to appreciate the load I'm carrying and put a little more effort into making things a bit easier for me. A little more help and attention here, folks!" Self-centeredness.

"I want to see what sex is like. I'm tired of waiting, or doing without. I don't think this relationship is going anywhere. It can just be casual, without any commitment issues or emotional baggage afterward. But I want some pleasure for myself." An evil desire within.

If we let it linger, if we stew over it, it starts to take over our thinking. It's like something has been conceived inside us, and now it's growing larger. And finally it comes out. We take action on it, it's born—and we've given birth to sin, as verse 15 says: "Then, after desire has conceived, it gives birth to sin."

But the process doesn't stop there, because the sin, once out in the open, continues to grow, and pretty soon it takes over our life, and the end result is ruin and devastation. Note the end of verse 15: "and sin, when it is full-grown, gives birth to death."

Once the sin is born, the sin itself grows and begins to take control of our life. Once we give birth and yield to the sin—once we pass off someone else's idea as our own, once we blow up and shred others around us, once we cross the line sexually—once the sin is born, it grows even larger and more dominating. At work, we begin to manipulate everything we can to get ahead on the job. At home, we're constantly making everybody walk on tip-toes to avoid our anger. On dates, we ignore everything about the inner life of the other person, and our only focus is on getting more sex each time we're together.

The sin that was born, grows, and becomes an adult, dominating our life. And within a short time, this full-grown sin gives birth to something else—it gives birth to death, a dying inside. A shriveling, sickening, deadening inside. We become disgusted with ourselves—how we're acting at work, or at home, or on dates. We're eaten away with guilt, we're fighting depression, we're dying inside.

How can we guard ourselves from this happening to us? How can we protect ourselves from this process, so that we keep the trial from becoming a temptation?

James gives us four steps. The first step is to be absolutely convinced that God has only something very good in mind with the trial. Whatever trial we're experiencing—a plateaued career, an overloaded schedule, a prolonged singleness—whatever set of circumstances we find ourselves in, we must start with the conviction that everything about God is absolutely good, totally good, fully good, nothing but good:

> *Don't be deceived, my dear brothers and sisters. Every good and perfect gift is from above, coming down from the Father of the heavenly lights, who does not change like shifting shadows. He chose to give us birth through the word of truth, that we might be a kind of firstfruits of all he created.* (1:16–18)

Everything that God is doing in your life is good. He's only thinking of what good and perfect gifts he can give you. *Good* gifts are superlative ones, expensive ones. *Perfect* gifts are ones that would uniquely suit you; they are chosen especially with you in mind.

When you think about giving a gift to someone you love, you want to give a good gift—top quality, not cheap or flimsy, but a name brand. A *good* gift. And you want to give a *perfect* gift—a gift uniquely and exactly suited to that particular person. Not golf clubs, because you know your friend doesn't play golf; but instead a titanium racquet to take her tennis game to the next level. A *perfect* gift. You start with the conviction that whatever God is doing in your life, it's a good and perfect gift—top of the line, and chosen especially for you.

A plateaued career? Maybe that's to get you to transfer to another company, because in a couple of months this one will suddenly tank. Or maybe it's to open your thinking to other lines of work that will be even more fascinating to you, and much more fun to do. Whatever the trial is, God only has something good in mind through it.

An overloaded schedule? Maybe it's to develop even more efficient work habits, and to feel good about your accomplishments, and to encourage others in their struggles. Whatever is happening, God is only working something good through it.

A prolonged singleness? Maybe it's to free you to be attentive to your parents during a time of need, or maybe it's to keep you available and ready for someone God is bringing to you in about a year. Whatever the circumstances, there's a good and perfect gift in them for you.

Everything God does is good, full of light and joy. He is "the Father of the heavenly lights." He's the one who created light. That's how he lives—in the light. Everything about him is bright, out in the open. And nothing's ever going to interfere with that good and perfect light coming to you. No shifting shadows. No clouds getting in the way, blocking the light from you, causing shadows or uncertainties about his good intentions.

Don't ever let yourself be deceived. God loves you. Passionately, joyfully, incredibly, he loves you. And every thought he has toward you is good. Whatever's happening in your life, there's something very good that he's working in you. The proof of this incredible love is that he chose you for himself, to give you eternal life with him. He chose you to be part of his family forever. Verse 18 tells us: "He chose to give us birth through the word of truth."

And someday you're going to be at the center of God's entire creation. The end of verse 18 says so: "that we might be a kind of firstfruits of all he created." A *firstfruit* is the one most eagerly awaited, the one most specially chosen. You—the pinnacle of God's creation. That's the overwhelming glory he has planned for you. Love. Incredible love. Nothing but good.

So the first step to keep the trial from becoming a temptation is to be absolutely convinced that whatever is happening in your life, God has only something good in mind through it.

Then, second, give thought to what that good might be. Resist any thought of becoming frustrated or angry with God, and instead look for what the good is that he may be doing. Ask him to show you what he's up to, and guard yourself from any impatience or complaints against him:

> My dear brothers and sisters, take note of this: Everyone should be quick to listen, slow to speak and slow to become angry, because human anger does not produce the righteousness that God desires. (1:19–20)

The second step to keep the trial from becoming a temptation is to be quick to listen to whatever wisdom God gives us. Be slow to complain against him. Be slow to become angry with him over what's happening, because an angry, complaining spirit will never bring about the good he's trying to do. Be quick to listen, slow to anger. "Father, show me what you're doing with my career. I'm trusting myself to your hands." "Lord, show me how to handle my schedule, instead of being overwhelmed by it." "Father, you know my desire to be married and to love. Give me some idea of your plans for me." Be quick to listen, slow to complain, slow to become angry.

And then third, if the temptation does start to arise, recognize what's causing it. Pin down the source—the self-centeredness that's causing it. Identify the evil that's still so prevalent in each of us. And then reject it. When an evil, self-centered desire pops into your mind, put it down, send it away, get rid of it:

> *Therefore, get rid of all moral filth and the evil that is so prevalent.* (1:21a)

"Father, my frustration over my career is because of my impatience and lack of trust. I don't want to be like that." "Lord, my anger over the computer or the house and kids or the missing suit and shirts, is because I want people to think about me and do things my way. I don't want to be that way." "Lord, going after sex is simply to gratify myself without regard for what it's doing to the other person or the relationship. That's not right." Identify the self-centeredness, the evil, and get rid of it.

And then finally, come back to the Word of God that has been planted in you, and that can take you safely through the trial. Humbly and obediently accept the wisdom that comes from the Scriptures, and this will guide you through the trial:

> *Therefore, get rid of all moral filth and the evil that is so prevalent, and humbly accept the word planted in you, which can save you.* (1:21)

When James says that the Word "can save you," he's not looking at our eternal salvation. He's looking at our being presently saved from temptation and sin. His meaning is, "Let the Word of God guide you so that you can safely arrive at the goal God has in mind."

"Accept the word, planted in you, which can save you." Accept the Word which says that God is in control of your career, that he planned all of your days even before you were born, and that he has prepared in advance all the good works you will do (Ps. 139:16; Eph. 2:10).

Accept the Word which says that God will never give you a schedule that is more than you can handle, that no set of circumstances will ever come your way except what is common to human experience. Accept that God promises he will never bring anything that is more than he knows you can manage, but will provide a way in which you can put your hand in his, and move through your circumstances without sin or devastation (1 Cor. 10:13).

Accept the Word which says that the marriage bed is undefiled, that sex within marriage is pure and honored, but that sex outside of marriage—fornication and adultery—leads to God's judgment (Heb. 13:4). Hear the promise of the Word, which says, "Blessed are the pure in heart, for they will see God" (Matt. 5:8).

When you're going through a trial, hang on to the conviction that God is doing something good in your life. Be quick to look for what that may be. Recognize that any temptation to sin comes from some self-centeredness inside of you. Put away that evil. And then humbly come to the Word of God. Open up its truth and let it guide you safely through the trial to the wonderful reward your God has for you.

4

THE MIRROR

James 1:22–27

For the past month there's been a warning light on my car dashboard: "Maintenance Required." This warning light means I'm overdue for a lube job and oil change. And, unless I take care of it, there's going to be some wear and tear on the engine.

Every time I start the car, this light comes on: "Maintenance Required." But at that moment I'm usually in a hurry to get somewhere—I need to be on campus; I'm meeting someone for lunch—so I don't do anything about it right then. When it comes on again at the end of the day, I'm on the way home, and it's too late since the garage will soon close.

What I need to do is to take the car in on my day off. But lots of times on my day off I never get in the car, and I forget that the warning light is there. As a result, weeks go by, and the car never gets taken care of.

The warning light tells me what to do, but because I don't do something about it right then, I quickly forget, and the wear and tear on the car continues.

Fortunately, one past week while I was in Canada, my wife, Nell, drove my car. And when she picked me up from the airport she said, "Your brakes are squealing; you probably need a brake job. I know you don't hear it when you're driving, but my hearing is better than yours. You ought to take the car to a garage to get the brakes checked." It's true that her hearing is better than mine. When we had small children at home and one of them would cry from the other room, and one of us needed to get up to see what was wrong, I never heard them. (At least, that's what I always told Nell.) Anyway, since the car repair had now escalated from lube and oil to brake job, I did finally remember to take it into the garage, and the warning light was taken care of.

Some of us men have a similar problem when we shave. We nick ourselves while shaving. To stop the bleeding, we put a little piece of tissue on our face. As we're looking in the mirror to see that the tissue is working, we say to ourselves, "I've got to make sure I take that off before I get to work." But we're out the door and gone, and once away from what the mirror tells us, we forget the tissue is there. If we don't do something when we see that we should, we forget, and we live with the consequences.

Seeing it in the mirror isn't enough. It's *doing* what the mirror tells you that changes things to the way things ought to be.

James has a similar point to make. "The Word of God," he says, "is like a mirror. Seeing what it says, listening to it, hearing the Word of God is not enough. It's *doing* it that brings you the blessing you want. If all you do is listen to the Word of God, but you don't actually do what it says, you're fooling yourself if you think that any blessing will come to your life. What you want out of life—strength, joy, wholeness—only comes when you actually do what the Bible says."

James is writing this to some friends of his. They're going through some difficult situations, some trials—tough economic times, strained relationships, uncertain futures. And he encourages them to hang in there. "God is using these trials," he says, "to bring good to your lives. And when he completes the process you'll feel like a crown has settled on your life."

"But in order for this to happen," he adds, "you must listen to what the Word of God says about how to get safely through the trial, and then you must act accordingly. As you go through the trial, hear what God says to do, and then actually do it. Then the blessing will come."

> Do not merely listen to the word, and so deceive yourselves. Do what it says. Anyone who listens to the word but does not do what it says is like someone who looks at his face in a mirror and, after looking at himself, goes away and immediately forgets what he looks like. But whoever looks intently into the perfect law that gives freedom, and continues in it—not forgetting what they have heard, but doing it—they will be blessed in what they do. (1:22–25)

The Word of God, James says, is like a mirror that tells you what you need to do. It's the perfect law that will guide you to freedom.

We don't usually think of laws as giving us freedom. Just the opposite, we think of laws as interfering with our freedom: I want to go in the carpool lane on the freeway, but the law says I'm not free to do that unless I have someone else in the car with me. I want to take my money out of my IRA because the value is going down, but the law says I can't do that without incurring a huge penalty. We tend to think of laws as interfering with our freedom.

But that's not always the case. Many times good laws actually lead to freedom. The laws about which side of the road to drive on, and which traffic-light color allows us to go through intersections—green, yellow, or red—actually create the freedom that lets us drive with safety. The laws of tennis—the serve must drop in between these lines, you can't take three bounces to return the ball—actually give us the freedom to enjoy the game. God's Word is like that—a law that gives freedom.

But it is a law. It's not advice. It's not a suggestion. It's not one possible option. It's a law. It's mandatory. Thankfully, however, it's a *perfect* law. It comes from a God who knows perfectly what we should do in each situation. He knows perfectly how we should act to get the wonderful life of freedom and blessing we want.

But to get that freedom, to get that blessing, we can't just listen to his law. We have to do it.

Sometimes we just listen to the Word. We come on Sunday. We listen to the Word of God. The Word says something about our marriage: "Husbands, give up your pride and selfishness for the sake of your wife." "Wives, yield and submit respectfully to your husbands." Or it says something about our schoolwork: "Don't turn in a paper you got off the Internet or from a friend." Or something about our giving: "Honor the Lord by writing substantial checks, something in the neighborhood of ten percent." Or something about our purity: "Cancel some of those cable channels; get some filters that will keep the porn sites off your computer."

We listen. We hear the Word. But we don't do anything about it. We don't do what it says. And we foolishly think that God is still going to bless us. James says we deceive ourselves.

Do not merely listen to the word, and so deceive yourselves. Do what it says. (1:22)

The blessing only comes when we do what the Word says.

But whoever looks intently into the perfect law that gives freedom, and continues in it—not forgetting what they have heard, but doing it— they will be blessed in what they do. (1:25)

What's the mirror telling you? About your marriage? Your schoolwork? Your giving? Your purity? Do you hear it? Don't merely listen. Do it. God's blessing—the crown, the wholeness of life—only comes when we do what the Word says.

In verses 26–27, James now summarizes the first section of his letter, and then previews the two sections that will follow. Verse 26 captures the first step of how to go successfully through our trials—don't deceive yourself by blaming God, but keep a tight rein on your tongue (1:13–26). Verse 27 then gives us the next two ways to act through trials so as to get God's reward—love your fellow believers who are going through similar distresses (which James will talk more about in chapter 2) and avoid the world's polluting ways of handling difficulties (which he will cover in chapters 3–5):

Those who consider themselves religious and yet do not keep a tight rein on their tongues deceive themselves, and their religion is worthless. Religion that God our Father accepts as pure and faultless is this: to look after orphans and widows in their distress and to keep oneself from being polluted by the world. (1:26–27)

If we consider ourselves religious—that is, if we consider ourselves seriously committed to God and his ways, eager to obey his Word and enjoy his blessing—then we must do what James has just been talking about. We must trust God's good purposes in our trials and obey what his Word tells us to do, rather than deceiving ourselves through mere listening or through blaming him angrily for our lapses. Further, those whose religion is genuinely pure and faultless—those whose lives are holy before God and blameless before men—will be committed both to loving others and to avoiding the world's ways of responding to difficulties.

In the biblical world, to look after orphans and widows was an idiom for loving the most unfortunate and needy in the community—the poor, the marginalized, those most in distress. James's former church members have all been going through trials in their new communities, but some have been more severely affected than others. The evidence of their genuine religion, James will say, the evidence of their deep belief that God is working good through their trials, is that they will impartially (2:1–13) and tangibly (2:14–26) love the poor believers in their midst. Chapter 2 will speak repeatedly of how our love for the most needy among us shows our own faith that God is in our trials.

Chapters 3–5 will then warn us against adopting the world's ways of handling difficulties (note how worldly or earthly behaviors repeatedly show up in this section; cf. 3:6,16; 4:4). When unbelievers are faced with stress or the possibility of persecution, their typical responses are to lash out against those they think are aggravating the difficulty (3:1–4:12) and to attempt to insulate themselves from further trouble by accumulating wealth (4:13–5:6). As we are gentle with others, and submissive to God's will, we avoid the world's polluting behaviors and eventually receive the promised blessing.

These are the thoughts that will occupy the rest of James's letter: If we love our fellow believers in their distress, and as we keep ourselves unspotted by the world, we will stand the test and receive the crown of life that the Lord has promised (1:12).

5

IMPARTIAL LOVE

James 2:1–13

Let's suppose two different families come to your church as visitors some Sunday.

If you were out on the driveway when the first family drove up, and watched their car go by, you would have looked at it rather enviously—expensive, new, shiny. "Somebody's doing OK to be able to afford that," you might say.

The car of the second family came right behind them. This car, well, you kind of heard it even before you saw it. You know—that noise that tells you, "This engine isn't long for this world." And when you looked at the car, it was old, rusty, with paint splotchy and faded, sides dented, trunk held down with rope, and the windows rolled down because the air-conditioning is broken. "Hmm, things must be tough for them. Low paying job. Probably hardly making it."

Both cars park, and the two families walk from the parking lot to the door of the church. You're getting your bulletin as they walk in, and you notice a difference in how the two families are dressed. The first family is in the latest styles, with well-tailored, coordinated outfits, and matching accessories. We're talking Nordstrom's all the way. The parents both look like they work out; they're fit and trim. It's obvious the woman's been to a hairdresser—she's frosted, styled, with attractive makeup. Their kids—a daughter in college, a son in high school—are well-dressed, poised, confident.

The second family is different. The man is in faded corduroys and an ill-fitting shirt. His shoes are scuffed, slanting to the sides because the heels are worn away, his shoelaces dragging. The woman is wearing a housedress. Her purse doesn't match it. Her hair needs work. Their kids are overweight, self-conscious, uncomfortable.

As the families are getting their bulletins, you suddenly realize you recognize someone in that first family. Maybe the man is the head of an engineering firm or a software company—a company you'd like to work for, or maybe sell something to. It'd be good to establish a contact with him for business reasons. Or maybe you recognize the wife as a professor at the university, someone who hires research assistants, and your daughter is applying for one of the grants in her department. Or maybe you recognize their high school son. You've seen his picture in the paper. He's the all-state quarterback for the local team. Might be kind of nice if he were part of the youth group. Or maybe their college daughter is beautiful, and your twenty-five-year-old son in grad school, standing next to you, is one of the leaders of the college group. You're sure he'd love to tell her about the group's activities, and maybe see that she gets to the college class and has a good time.

The second family, well, they're nobody you've ever seen before. You're not even sure they live in your bedroom community; maybe they're from one of the apartments in a nearby city.

Both families finally have their bulletins and walk into the back of the auditorium. One moves to the right, the other to the left. Both families stop and hesitate because they're not sure where they should sit. This is their first time at your church, and they're trying to get the lay of the land and figure out where they should go.

By now you also have come into the back of the auditorium, and you see both families, one on each side, both hesitating, trying to make up their minds what they should do. And it occurs to you that you could offer some help . . . to one family.

Which family do you go to? Which one do you walk toward? Which family do you give attention to?

You'd be tempted to go to the first family. "Hi, my name is Don Sunukjian. Can I help you? We don't save special seats here, so you can sit anywhere you want. My wife and I normally sit in this section—you can get a good view of the screen, and you can get to the donuts and coffee more quickly afterwards. Why don't you join us?"

You'd be tempted to go to that first family, because, well, you never know—it might lead to a job or a sale, or maybe a grant for your daughter, or a date for your son. You'd be drawn to the first family—they're attractive, and they might do something for you; you might benefit in some way.

Two families come into church. Which one would you help?

That's the question James poses in his letter to Christian friends he hadn't seen for fifteen years. As we noted earlier, James had been a pastor to these people at his church in Jerusalem, before they had fled the city due to persecution. Remember that for a time it had been too dangerous to be a Christian in Jerusalem. Many believers, including Stephen, were falsely charged and executed. So many families had fled to other cities and countries in order to start life over.

But in their new cities, they were often viewed with suspicion. They were immigrants, refugees, strangers. We noted before that they faced many seemingly insurmountable obstacles—lack of jobs, trouble getting business permits, harassment from local hooligans, being cheated in the markets and tormented at school. They were hated by everyone and found themselves isolated in the midst of a hostile society. On Sundays they gathered in their small church, a fragile minority, looking for comfort from each other in a menacing environment.

And their pastor James wrote to them, knowing their vulnerabilities and the many temptations that would come because of them. And so, as he writes, he imagines a Sunday when two first-time visitors might come to their church, two different men from the community, checking them out, each one maybe interested in attending the church for a time. One of the first-time visitors is obviously wealthy. The church members recognize him as an influential man in the community. The other visitor is the opposite; he is poor, and nobody knows him. And James raises the question for his friends, "Which one would you go to? Which one would you pay attention to?" Let's see how James describes these visitors, and his answer to the question he raises.

Here's James's introduction of the first visitor:

Suppose a man comes into your meeting wearing a gold ring and fine clothes. (2:2a)

A gold ring and fine clothes—that's the way the Romans of the ruling class were usually described. Our equivalent today might be a three-piece suit. Gold ring, fine clothes—that was the description of a government official, someone high up, someone who determined the laws and controlled the patronage jobs.

So the first visitor, James says, is a man of wealth and influence in the city—the kind of man who could get you a job or a permit. The kind of man who could get the hooligans to lay off. The kind of man who could see to it that your wife and kids were no longer hassled. The kind of man who could do something for you, benefit you in some way, make your troubles and trials go away.

The second visitor is poor and unknown. James describes him in verse 2 as "a poor man in filthy old clothes." His clothes are shabby, nondescript, and maybe even a little bit dirty, because soap was expensive in that day. He's poor and can't afford soap, so his clothes are grimy. They smell of sweat and earth.

Two first-time visitors—one wealthy and influential, the other poor and insignificant. Which one do you go to? Which one do you give attention to?

Do you give special attention to the rich one? That's what James visualizes in verse 3: "You show special attention to the man wearing fine clothes and say, 'Here's a good seat for you.'" "I've got a spot on the aisle for you, lots of leg-room, you can see well, get to the coffee fast." Do you pay special attention to the rich one, because he's the one who can do something for you?

And do you kind of brush off the poor one? Verse 3: "But say to the poor man, 'You stand there' or 'Sit on the floor by my feet.'" "There are some folding chairs over there you can set up." Or, "Here's a spot, over on the side, right under the loudspeaker." Do you ignore and brush off the poor man?

If you are really committed to following Christ, James says, if your belief in Christ is central to your life, and you find yourself in this situation—when the influential and insignificant, the attractive and unattractive, the rich and poor are both in your church—you must treat them absolutely the same. You must treat them equally, without thought of gain, without regard for any benefit you might receive. You must love them impartially, not for what you can get from them. If you are really committed to following Christ, you must not show favoritism.

That's what James stresses in verse 1: "My brothers and sisters, believers in our glorious Lord Jesus Christ must not show favoritism." Do not pay attention to people based on what they can do for you. Do not treat them differently based on what you might get from them. Be absolutely impartial. Love them equally.

Now why does James stress this? Why does James want us to be as ready to love the poor man as the rich man, as quick to pay attention to the insignificant as well as the influential? Why is it so important that we love impartially, without thought of gain? You might say, "Well, that's the right Christian thing to do. That's the way a Christian ought to act." And that would be true. But the reasons are much more profound than that; they go far deeper than, "It's the right thing to do." In the verses that follow, James probes and searches our hearts as he reveals four penetrating reasons why it's so important that we love impartially and without thought of gain.

First, he says, when you love impartially, without thought of gain, you show your deep trust in God—that he's the one who controls your circumstances, that he's the one who determines your future, not the rich and influential of this world. You show your conviction that God is the one who determines the good things that come to you, not men.

But if you show favoritism in your love, if you're partial to those you think can do something for you, then that shows you're not confident about God's role in your life. You're unsure, uncertain whether he's in control. You're wavering, vacillating, making distinctions between what God can handle and what men control. And because of your doubts about God, you're now deciding what you will do based on evil, self-centered motives. You're making judgments based on the idea of "who can do what for me." That's what James means in verse 4: When you show favoritism and pay special attention to the rich, "have you not discriminated among yourselves and become judges with evil thoughts?"

When James says, "have you not discriminated," the word *discriminated* is the same word he used earlier for "doubted" when he talked about asking

God for wisdom but doubting while you are doing it (1:5–6). Doubting, discriminating: the same word, meaning vacillating, wavering, making distinctions.

If you discriminate in your love, you reveal your doubts about whether God is in control. You've begun to judge the situation with evil thoughts: "God may not be in control of my job, my career, so I'd better play favorites with this executive, and ignore the other family." "God may not be in control of my children's future, so I need to be partial to these people who can hire them, or date them, and not worry about whether anyone is helping these other people." And because of your doubts about God, you judge the situation and decide what you will do based on evil, unworthy motives—not "What are the needs," but rather "Who can do what for me."

The first reason it's so important to love impartially, then, without thought of gain, is because it shows your deep confidence in God. There are no doubts, no distinctions. To love impartially shows your complete trust in God—that he is in control.

There's a second reason, James goes on to say, why you should love impartially. You must do so not only because it shows your trust in God, that he is in control, but also because it shows your wisdom about people— that it's often the poor who have the deepest walk with God. When you love without partiality, it's because you know that the poor are very often the ones who are most fully centered on God, whereas the rich often have no use for him in their lives. The poor are often the most spiritually rich, whereas the rich are often the most abusive and cruel. This is not a hard and fast rule, of course, but it is very often the case. Hear what James has to say:

> Listen, my dear brothers and sisters: Has not God chosen those who are poor in the eyes of the world to be rich in faith and to inherit the kingdom he promised those who love him? But you have dishonored the poor. Is it not the rich who are exploiting you? Are they not the ones who are dragging you into court? Are they not the ones who are blaspheming the noble name of him to whom you belong? (2:5–7)

If you dishonor or insult the poor person, if you shun him, you may be shunning someone that God has chosen and is very close to, someone who has a rich and deep walk with him. You may be shunning a man who daily walks with God in faith, a man who looks to God every morning, asking that God will keep his car running because there's no money for repairs. And every night he returns to God and thanks him for making it through another day.

If you dishonor the poor person, you may be shunning a housewife who doesn't have money to put her elderly mother in a care facility. So she's taking care of her mother in her own home, and every day she looks to God to keep her loving and gentle and patient.

If you insult the poor person, you may brushing off the single mother that God is filling with grace every day, helping her keep up with trips to daycare, with her job, with the grocery shopping, the hurried meals, the baths, the homework. And then, at night, when she's overcome with weariness and tears and loneliness, he's loving her and consoling her and assuring her of his presence and protection.

When you dishonor the poor person, you may be dishonoring the shy teenager who doesn't say much, isn't an athlete or a student leader, but who works at McDonald's after school and quietly gives one-half of his earnings to feed orphans in India.

Often it's the poor who have the richest and deepest walk with God, and to love them quickly and fully is to enter into the life of someone God has chosen, to see their deep walk with him.

On the other hand, to show favoritism to the rich can be a fool's errand, for they are often the most abusive and cruel.

> *Is it not the rich who are exploiting you? Are they not the ones who are dragging you into court? Are they not the ones who are blaspheming the noble name of him to whom you belong?* (2:6b–7)

Is the Fortune-500 executive going to do you good? Or is he going to use you for anything he can, and then spit you out? Ask his ex-wives. Ask his serial girlfriends, his business lackeys. Is it the rich or the poor who cause the business scandals, drag firms into bankruptcy, and destroy investors while building personal mansions? Is it the rich or the poor who take advantage of you in court because they have the deep pockets to hire the lawyers and beat you back? Is it the rich or the poor who use their good-old-boy networks to get insider tips, government contracts, preferential treatment, and company perks? Is it the rich or the poor who smile to your face and do a hatchet job to your back, who show up at church for image purposes, but never let it affect their lives in any way?

Of course, not all rich people are this way. And many poor people also commit crimes out of necessity or greed or other reasons. But James's point here is that more often the rich are the ones who have no use for God in their lives. Therefore, when you love impartially, you show your wisdom about people—that it's often the poor who have the deepest walk with God.

There's a third reason, James says, why you should love impartially: because it shows your submission to Scripture, that you will obey it to the fullest extent. It shows that you want to be fully obedient to *all* that God has said. When you obey *this* command—the command to love, which is the supreme command—you show your willingness to obey *all* of God's commands.

But if we disobey this command, the greatest and most important of all commands, we're saying to God, "I don't care what you say, I'm going to do what I want. I don't care what your Word says, I'll break any of your laws if I feel like it or if I think it will serve my purposes." If we break this greatest command—the command to love—we reveal deep down that our heart is not submissive to God, and that we will break or transgress any of his laws whenever it suits us.

If you really keep the royal law found in Scripture—that is, the supreme law, the law that means the most to our King, the greatest law he gave, the law that says, "Love your neighbor as yourself"—you are doing right. That is, you are revealing your desire to keep all of God's commands, to obey him in every way. "But if you show favoritism"—that is, if you break this law— "you sin and are convicted by the law as lawbreakers. For whoever keeps the whole law and yet stumbles at just one point is guilty of breaking all of it. For he who said, 'You shall not commit adultery,' also said, 'You shall not murder.' If you do not commit adultery but do commit murder, you have become a lawbreaker." (2:8–11)

Whoever keeps the whole law—that is, whoever says, "Yeah, I'll do what God says"—and yet stumbles at just one point—"Oh, except for that one thing, I'm not going to do that"—reveals a rebellious spirit and shows that deep down he is prepared to break or transgress *any* command whenever it suits him. Whoever stumbles at just one point, is guilty of breaking all of it, because God views his Word, his commands, like a pane of glass— you can't break one part of it without shattering the whole. To deliberately break one of God's laws is to essentially say, "I'll disobey any law whenever I want to."

And this attitude makes you guilty before God. God sees the Scripture as an unbreakable whole, as his perfect and entire will for our lives. "For he who said, 'You shall not commit adultery,' also said, 'You shall not murder.' If you do not commit adultery but do commit murder"—if you pick and choose among God's commands—you reveal that you are willing to rebel against him, and "you have become a lawbreaker," unsubmissive to his will. Love impartially, James says, without thought of gain, because this shows that your whole life is submitted to God's Word, and that you want to obey him in every way you can.

Finally, James says, there's one last reason why you should love impartially: it shows your dependence on God's grace, that you need his mercy toward you to be greater than his judgment of you. To show mercy toward others, to love them without making judgments about how deserving they are, is to acknowledge that you too want God's mercy toward you to be greater than, stronger than, triumphing over, his judgment of you. We should love others impartially, James says, because this will determine whether God gives us the judgment we deserve, or loves us with infinite mercy.

> *Speak and act as those who are going to be judged by the law that gives freedom, because judgment without mercy will be shown to anyone who has not been merciful. Mercy triumphs over judgment.* (2:12–13)

Speak and act according to this law of impartial love, for your obedience to this law becomes the basis for how God will act toward you. This law of liberty, this command to love impartially, this command that makes you free—free to trust God's control in your life, free to focus on those whom he has chosen and who have the deepest walk with him, free to obey all that he has written in his Word—this command to show mercy to others without regard of gain, is what determines whether God, in return, will continually stream mercy into your life, or whether he will give you the justice you deserve.

Maybe next Sunday you'll find yourself near someone who looks out of place, alone, uncertain. Maybe it's a young couple in the parking lot, struggling to get all their gear and small children together. Maybe it's an elderly person walking slowly with a cane, hoping not to get bumped, trying to open a door. Maybe it's a teenager with skin problems and shirttail flapping. Maybe it's someone who weighs too much, or talks too loud, or smells too strong. But here, among God's people, they are loved. Loved for who they are, and not for what they can do. Loved without thought of gain, because God is in control of our life. Loved because unknown to us God may be doing wonderful things in their lives. Loved because our greatest desire is to obey all that God has said. Loved because we also are aware that, though we are unworthy, God's mercy and love has never ceased from our own lives.

Here, among God's people, there's no favoring one over another, there's only impartial love.

6

LIVING, LOVING, LASTING FAITH

James 2:14–26

How can you know whether you'll walk successfully with God through a trial? When trouble hits with full force, how can you know whether you'll move safely through it without sinning or being devastated by it? God promises a crown of life if we persevere through trials, trusting him to work good in us through them (1:12). How can you know whether you'll persevere or become unglued, whether you'll trust or fall apart?

If you go through a long stretch of unemployment, will you be able to hang in there confidently, or will you become frantic and desperate? If you have to care for an elderly parent over a long period of time, will you stay sweet-spirited and look for the bright spots in your care-giving tasks? Or will you resent it bitterly, lash out against your parent, and make life miserable for everyone concerned? If you don't get into the college or grad school that you want, will you still believe that God's good hand is shaping your life? Or will you say, "It's the pits. Nothing's going right. My life's over"? If a situation at work becomes difficult or unpleasant because of the people involved, if your career plateaus, if an accident or illness permanently affects your family, will you have the faith to persevere, or will you descend into seething and self-pity?

James says there's a way you can look at your faith now and know whether it is the kind of faith that will stand the test and receive the reward. There's a way you can know whether your faith is alive and vital, and will see you through the trial to the good end that God intends.

Here's how you know, James says: Your loving deeds toward others reveal a living faith. Your loving acts of compassion and mercy show that you have a genuine trusting faith that will see you through the trials to God's reward.

> *What good is it, my brothers and sisters, if someone claims to have faith but has no deeds? Can such faith save them? Suppose a brother or a sister is without clothes and daily food. If one of you says to them, "Go in peace; keep warm and well fed," but does nothing about their physical needs, what good is it? In the same way, faith by itself, if it is not accompanied by action, is dead.* (2:14–17)

We need to understand some of the words James is using, for in the Bible they can often refer to more than one thing. First of all, when James asks, "Can such faith save them?" he's not looking at your eternal salvation. He's looking at being taken safely through your trials, being delivered from sinning during your prolonged troubles. Earlier he had said that you "should accept the word planted in you, which can save you" (1:21), meaning that God's Word would safely guide you through temptation; it would save or deliver you from becoming angry with God. His thought here is similar: he's looking at the quality or nature of your faith that will safely take you through your trials.

Secondly, the faith he has in mind is not faith in Jesus Christ as Savior. It's faith that God is working good in you through your trials. It's the vital, trusting faith that submits humbly to what God is doing, and as a result will stand the test and receive the reward.

James's thought is that we can know we have the kind of faith that will safely take us through our trials to God's good reward if we see ourselves doing good deeds of love and compassion to others. On the other hand, if we claim to be trusting God through our trials, but at the same time are ignoring the worse plight of others, our claim is false—our faith is *dead*, useless, impotent to carry us through our own difficulties. The faith that is alive, genuine, and persevering is the faith that cares lovingly for the tangible needs of others.

As an example of loving deeds toward others, James supposes that "a brother or a sister is without clothes and daily food." James is not talking here about a panhandler who confronts us on the street, or a person with a sign at the end of a freeway ramp, or a homeless person in a park. He's not talking about strangers to whom we may or may not respond; he's talking about fellow believers who are in distress as a result of the trials that have fallen on the congregation. They are in the category of "the orphans and widows in their distress" that he mentioned earlier (1:27).

To say that such fellow believers are without clothes and daily food means that the only clothes they own are the ones on their backs and that they don't know where their next meal is coming from. Merely to say to those with such great needs, "Go in peace; keep warm and well fed"—basically, "It's been nice talking to you; take care; see you around; have a nice day; good luck to you"—is to reveal a dead faith, one that essentially discounts God's presence in the congregation's common trials. Can such faith save them? No. "What good is it?" James asks twice. It is useless (2:20). A faith divorced from tangible acts of mercy and compassion is insufficient to take you safely through your own trials.

The reason this is true—that loving acts reveal a faith that will sustain us through trials—is because, as James said earlier, if we are willing to obey the greatest command to love, even to our potential loss, then we will be willing to obey any other command that may be necessary to persevere successfully (2:1–12). If you are willing to "keep the royal law found in Scripture, 'Love your neighbor as yourself,'" then you will be willing to obey all of God's commands, and because of this you will persevere.

At this point, James imagines that someone objects to his assertion that faith must be accompanied by tangible good deeds in order to be genuine and useful to us personally. "But someone will say, 'You have faith; I have deeds.'" (2:18a). The objector counters, "It's possible for one person to have faith that God is working through trials and not have loving deeds to others, while another person acts lovingly toward others without necessarily trusting God's presence in the trials. The two don't have to go together."

James's response is to offer three biblical examples to prove the necessary connection between faith and deeds—that unless faith in God's working is accompanied by tangible acts, it's a meaningless, dead faith. His first example is a negative one:

> Show me your faith without deeds, and I will show you my faith by my deeds. You believe that there is one God. Good! Even the demons believe that—and shudder. (2:18b–19)

The demons believe that there is one God—they have a kind of faith. But since they are totally devoid of good deeds, they shudder, because they know their faith is useless and dead, and that they are doomed. They have never shown love or mercy to anyone, and because "judgment without mercy will be shown to anyone who has not been merciful" (2:13), they will be destroyed. There is no genuine faith without good deeds.

James's next two examples are positive: Abraham and Rahab both showed their genuine faith through trials by tangible deeds of obedience:

> You foolish person, do you want evidence that faith without deeds is useless? Was not our father Abraham considered righteous for what he did when he offered his son Isaac on the altar? You see that his faith and his actions were working together, and his faith was made complete by what he did. And the scripture was fulfilled that says, "Abraham believed God, and it was credited to him as righteousness," and he was called God's friend. You see that a person is considered righteous by what they do and not by faith alone.
>
> In the same way, was not even Rahab the prostitute considered righteous for what she did when she gave lodging to the spies and sent them off in a different direction? As the body without the spirit is dead, so faith without deeds is dead. (2:20–26)

We know from Genesis that Abraham had faith—he believed God when God promised him descendants without number, even though he was then childless:

> After this, the word of the LORD came to Abram in a vision:
> "Do not be afraid, Abram.
>   I am your shield,
>   your very great reward.
>
> But Abram said, "Sovereign LORD, what can you give me since I remain childless and the one who will inherit my estate is Eliezer of Damascus?" And Abram said, "You have given me no children; so a servant in my household will be my heir."

> Then the word of the LORD came to him: "This man will not be your heir, but a son who is your own flesh and blood will be your heir." He took him outside and said, "Look up at the sky and count the stars—if indeed you can count them." Then he said to him, "So shall your offspring be."
>
> Abram believed the LORD, and he credited it to him as righteousness. (Gen. 15:1–6)

At that moment of belief, God initially credited Abraham with a genuine righteous faith. But thirty years later Abraham demonstrated the reality of that faith through a deed of concrete obedience when he willingly offered his son Isaac on the altar—his only son, the son who was essential to God's promise. Through this tangible act, James says, "His faith and his actions were working together, and his faith was made complete by what he did." And the Scripture's earlier pronouncement of Abraham's righteousness was fulfilled. This living faith then carried Abraham safely through the years to the "crown of life" (James 1:12) that he received—the honor of being called God's friend (cf. 2 Chron. 20:7; Isa. 41:18).

Similarly, the prostitute Rahab claimed to have faith that God would deliver fortified Jericho and the entire land of Canaan to the invading Israelites:

> Before the spies lay down for the night, she went up on the roof and said to them, "I know that the LORD has given you this land and that a great fear of you has fallen on us, so that all who live in this country are melting in fear because of you. We have heard how the LORD dried up the water of the Red Sea for you when you came out of Egypt, and what you did to Sihon and Og, the two kings of the Amorites east of the Jordan, whom you completely destroyed. When we heard of it, our hearts melted in fear and everyone's courage failed because of you, for the LORD your God is God in heaven above and on the earth below." (Josh. 2:8–11)

The proof that her claim was genuine—that she had a living faith that would safely take her through the city's destruction—was shown by her concrete deed "when she gave lodging to the spies and sent them off in a different direction." James has demonstrated his point: "As the body without the spirit is dead, so faith without deeds is dead." You know that your faith in God's goodness is alive, and that it will safely carry you through life's trials, if it is accompanied by concrete deeds of obedience.

Nell and I once had a neighbor named Gretchen. She and her husband were members of our church. Gretchen had a car she wanted to sell. An international student with small children responded to her ad. The student didn't have much money, but he did have enough for the quoted price of the car. Gretchen agreed to sell the car to him, but asked for a couple of days. She knew that the tires on the car were wearing thin, and was concerned for the safety of the small children. But she also knew that the student didn't have the money to do anything about them. So, she bought new tires for the car, paid for the appropriate inspection sticker, and then delivered the car to the student for the original quoted price. Loving deeds proved the reality of her faith.

Our concrete acts may not be as dramatic as Abraham's or Rahab's, but they can still demonstrate a living faith. It can be as simple as calling an elderly, lonely relative and talking for half an hour. Or taking the kids of a single mom for a day so that she can have some time for herself. Maybe it's helping a friend move, or fixing a screen for a widow, or cleaning the house of a sick friend.

I'm not real good at some of these handy-man things. But I believe my faith is real and has carried me through significant trials because of the tangible deeds I do seem able to do. Often my deeds involve anonymous gifts of money to someone in great need. Once during the 1980s a dear Christian friend encountered heavy uninsured medical bills. I knew this person had little money. Anonymously, I managed to leave an envelope containing $1,000 on his car seat, with an unsigned note that said, "You're a dear brother. God bless you." (And that's when $1,000 was worth a lot more than it is today.) I say that not to pat myself on the back, but just to show that that's how this sort of thing sometimes shows up in my life.

What about you? Do your loving deeds reveal a living faith that will take you through your trials to God's reward?

7

TONGUE IN CHECK

James 3:1-12

Sometimes as Christians we feel that we're not being treated fairly by the media. They seem hostile to us. They don't describe us honestly. They give us unattractive labels, lump us in with weirdoes and extremists, and then shoot us down with cheap shots.

For example, if there's a school board meeting or a PTA meeting to talk about a sex education program in the high school, and if some Christians at the meeting come to the microphone to urge an "abstinence only" program, you know somebody's going to write to the paper the next day that, "These Christians are out of touch with reality. They haven't a clue what's going on in the real world. They should quit trying to force their morality on everyone else." And you sense the hostility.

If the subject is abortion, some newspaper reporter will inevitably interview and quote someone who is "incensed" at the Christian viewpoint. "Who are these people who think they can tell a woman what she can and can't do? They're the ones who bomb the clinics and shoot the abortion doctors. They're dangerous." And we're lumped in with extremists.

If the subject is homosexuality or gay marriage, we're accused of intolerance, discrimination, and homophobia. And they jab at us, "Where are those wonderful Christian virtues you're supposed to have; you know—love, acceptance, and 'judge not lest ye be judged'?" Kind of a cheap shot.

In a local school district a few years ago, three Christian school board members refused to accept the State's definition of "gender." They had moral objections to the way gender was defined. State officials threatened to withhold $40 million from the school district, and even to take over the schools if the Board didn't back down. The Christian members held their ground, and eventually got a new, acceptable definition. But letters to the editor showed up in the local newspaper that characterized the Christian board members like this:

> Religious fundamentalists . . . of all stripes are a danger to the Western way of life. . . .
>
> What is really going on in the . . . district is about a clique of Christians persecuting a group. . . .
>
> The morality police are at it again. The majority . . . are abusing their position to further a radical "religio-political" agenda. . . . These board members must be recalled.

Even if the issue is as simple as the role of a husband and wife in marriage, and we try to explain the biblical guidelines of love and yieldedness—guidelines that we know will produce the happiest marriages and the most stable families—and even if we explain this biblical teaching in as clear and gentle a manner as possible, we're accused of being anti-feminist, chauvinistic, and politically incorrect. The media and the culture have a bias against us. And out of this bias, they have come up with a handy label for us. Out of this hostility, they have come up with a label that pigeon-holes us, isolates us, and sounds the alarm against us.

You know what the label is? You know who we are? We are the "Religious Right." Or, if you prefer, "Right-Wing Fundamentalists." Yep, that's who we are—the Religious Right. And according to our secular culture, we're a scary group. "Watch out for the Religious Right. They're weird. They're dangerous. Watch out for them. Don't let them take over." The media and our culture want to brand us as fringe, foolish, and fanatic—an unattractive minority, anti-intellectuals, a menace to the American way of life.

And if people get it into their minds that *you* are part of such a group, if they conclude somehow that you are part of the "Religious Right," it could cause you problems. It could create difficulties for you. It could affect whether they hire you, or promote you, or do business with you. It could affect whether they give you a good grade in a course, or advance you through graduate school. It could affect whether they develop a friendship with you, or date you, or act neighborly with you.

Now what should we do about this? What should we do about this media bias and cultural hostility? How can we counter this unfair label—the Religious Right? What's the answer?

(Descend the steps, move among the aisles, and continue in angry accusatory tones, pointing to different segments of the audience for each of the following paragraphs.)

I'll tell you what the answer is! I'll tell you what we should do about it!

The problem is, some of you *are* anti-intellectual. You get up and spout off opinions without any facts. You're abrasive and argumentative. You're not reasonable. You don't give and take. You don't seem to be able to settle for small gains. You've got to have all or nothing. You want to win the battle, but you end up losing the war. You go about the whole process wrong, and give the rest of us a bad name.

Listen to me! You need to stop some of your inflammatory activities—your protests, your rallies. That's not being smart. You're aggravating the situation. You're just giving the other side more ammunition, confirming their opinion. And making it difficult for the rest of us. I'm a Christian too, and I don't like getting called names.

Come on, really! There's a time and place for everything. Concentrate first on establishing relationships. Make yourself credible, become accepted as a reasonable human being. Show them you're competent, show them you're capable, that you can cut the mustard professionally or academically. Then, maybe somewhere down the line, there'll be small ways that you can bring in some of these other things.

But what do you expect? When you hit them head-on, out of the blue, before they're ready for it—no wonder they get gun-shy and antsy and hostile. And we all pay the penalty.

I'll tell you what the problem is! Some of you are just not thinking how a Christian ought to be. And what you need to do is . . . *(pause)*

At this point you probably want to say, "Don, wait a minute. Stop. Stop. What are you doing? You're angry with us. You're accusing us. You're abusing us. Your words are not helping, they're hurting. You're sinning against us."

And you would be right. I would be sinning against you.

If I sense a danger with our being called the "Religious Right," if I see the difficulties that label could cause all of us, the problems that might come from that, and I start telling you what to do—the chances are that my words would wound, that my tongue would sin against you. If I'm worried that the actions of other Christians might cause me to suffer, and I'm all too ready to *teach* them what to do to prevent that from happening, the chances are great that I will sin as I speak.

That's why James tells the believers to whom he is writing, "When you find yourself being affected by the actions of other believers in your church, don't be too quick to step forward as a 'teacher,' instructing others what to do, for you are too likely to sin in the process. I know you're facing difficulties. I know that the actions of some believers, though well meaning, are aggravating the difficulties. But don't be too quick to advise them what they should do, because you probably won't be able to control your tongue. The only people who should try to tell others what to do are those who are in control of all areas of their own lives. Only someone of spiritual depth and maturity, someone who has the rest of his life in control should presume to 'teach' others how to act in these difficult situations." That's the warning James gives:

> Not many of you should become teachers, my fellow believers, because
> you know that we who teach will be judged more strictly. We all stumble
> in many ways. Anyone who is never at fault in what they say is perfect,
> able to keep their whole body in check. (3:1–2)

James's words have often been explained incorrectly as a warning against becoming a Bible teacher in the local church. Ironically, the speaker giving the warning is usually a Bible teacher telling other believers not to become Bible teachers. In other words, "Don't become a pastor or Sunday school teacher or small group leader." Apart from the irony of this, this explanation also seems contrary to all the biblical passages which speak highly of biblical teachers. They are among God's gifts to the church (Rom. 12:7; 1 Cor. 12:28; Eph. 4:11). We're told to seek out those who are capable of teaching; Paul tells Timothy to entrust his teachings "to reliable people who will also be qualified to teach others" (2 Tim. 2:2).

James's words have nothing to do with teaching Scripture or biblical doctrine. Instead, his warning is against presuming to teach others how they should act so that they don't add to the stresses and hardships that the rest of us are facing. It's a warning against presuming to instruct others as to how they can stop causing trials for the rest of us. His words continue the theme that has occupied his whole letter—the theme of how to act in trials, how to act when we face difficult and stressful situations.

As we've noted before, he's writing to Jewish Christians who are facing different kinds of trials. They're former members of his church who were driven from their homes and cities. And now they're scattered in different localities and countries, trying to start life over in new communities. And they're having a tough go of it. They're being resented and discriminated against. It's one trial after another—finding housing, getting a job, avoiding hassles, learning the local customs. The purpose of James's whole letter is to tell them how to face these trials. That's the focus of his whole book is on how to act when we find ourselves in stressful and difficult situations.

He's told us to consider it pure joy when we experience these trials, because through them we are becoming mature and complete, not lacking anything, as long as we don't become angry with God (chapter 1). He's encouraged us to love one another during the trials—impartially and tangibly—for this will reveal a genuine trusting faith that will safely take us through the trials (chapter 2).

Now he takes up his next point: While we're going through these trials, we must avoid being infected or polluted by how the world would do things. We must not adopt the world's attitudes and coping mechanisms. This is what he will emphasize from chapter 3 through chapter 5—don't talk or act as the world would talk or act during a trial.

All through these chapters James will mention the world frequently. He will talk about how the world gets into us. He will talk about how the world's wisdom is the opposite from God's wisdom. He will warn against friendship with the world. And his continual emphasis will be: Don't let the world's way of doing things influence what you say or how you act in the midst of a trial.

So, in chapter 3, he takes up a typical way someone in the world would react to a trial—by reaming out others who are supposedly contributing to the group's difficulties by their actions, lashing out too quickly against others with angry advice about how they can stop adding to the stresses and hardship by their behavior. The reason James brings this up is because sometimes our trials may be due to the behavior of other Christians. Sometimes the actions of other believers, though well meaning, can cause difficulties for the rest of us.

For example, it could be Christian parents who don't let their child play soccer or Little League on Sundays. As a result, if the Christian kid is a good athlete, the team doesn't win as many games as they might on Sundays. And the other parents get ticked off, and they gripe to us about the boy's parents, and include us in their hostile judgment: "You religious people cost us the tournament. We could have gone to State." And we find ourselves awkwardly trying to explain or apologize to them. The well-meaning actions of some can cause difficulties for the rest of us.

It could be at school, in a classroom. A Christian student has the courage to speak up for his views. He has the courage, but unfortunately he doesn't have the facts or ability to hold his own in the give-and-take discussion. Within a few minutes he ends up humiliated in the class and silenced, and the rest of the Christians are embarrassed that he made our position look foolish and unfounded. His actions make us look bad.

It could be at work, in the office. Maybe it's a Christian who is a bit too insistent in his witnessing, taking advantage of any comment or incident that happens in the office to bring up the Lord or the Bible. But instead of winning people over, he's turning them off. They're avoiding him. And we get caught in guilt by association; people are putting their guard up around us too because they know we believe the same things the other Christian does.

It could be Christian relatives who throw a damper on the holiday gatherings of the family. They arrive late to the gathering, making everybody wait to eat. The reason they're late is because there was some church service they wanted to attend. When they get there and see the alcohol being served, they indicate their displeasure with frowns and faces. When the meal is served and the non-Christians start eating, one of the Christians interrupts and asks, "Can I offer a prayer to bless the food before we eat?" And the non-Christians awkwardly put down their utensils with embarrassed glances. And we feel these relatives are doing the cause of Christ more damage than good, and we're getting lumped in with them.

Sometimes other Christians add to the trials and stresses of our life. And our tendency is to want to slap them a bit and tell them to "shape up, get smart." But in such situations, James says, "Don't be too quick to tell others what they ought to do. Don't be too quick to instruct others how they should act. Don't presume too quickly to become a teacher to them." That's his caution, his warning to go slow. "Not many of you should become teachers."

Now, why does he say that? Why does he caution us to avoid giving advice or making a speech in such a situation? In the verses that follow, he first gives a bottom-line answer, and then he explains what he means. He first gives a short-form, summary answer, and then he spells it out in more detail.

His bottom-line, short-form answer is: We should not presume to be teachers because it's too likely we will sin with our words. We should not presume to be teachers because the chances are too great that we will stumble with our tongues, that in the process of telling others what to do, we will sin against them, and thus incur God's judgment. The only people who should think of teaching in such situations, James says, is someone who is in control of all other areas of their lives. And that's a level of maturity that not many have. Look again at verses 1–2. "Not many of you should become teachers, my fellow believers, because you know that" as we presume to counsel or teach there is too great a chance that we will sin with our tongues, and "we who teach will be judged more strictly. We all stumble in many ways." We all sin in many ways. But the easiest way to sin, the most common, and the hardest sin to prevent, is with the tongue. "Anyone who is never at fault in what they say is perfect." Only the person who can avoid stumbling or sinning with his tongue is perfect—perfect in the sense of spiritually mature, *complete*—someone who is already close to what God wants us to be (1:4)—someone who is "able to keep their whole body in check," someone who is in control of all areas of his life, and therefore able to control his tongue.

Don't presume to be a teacher, because to do so without sinning and being judged takes a level of maturity that not many have. That's his short-form answer.

Then, in verses 3–12 James explains what he means by this summary answer. He breaks it down and goes through it in more detail. He shows why it's true that because it's so likely we will sin with our tongues, we should avoid teaching others until we see a consistent maturity in our lives and an ability to control all areas.

As he explains in these verses, James will develop four thoughts, four statements:

1. When we are in control of our tongues, we can accomplish great things. (vv. 3–5a)
2. But when we are not in control of our tongues, we can cause great damage. (vv. 5b–6)
3. Unfortunately, the sad truth is that very few of us have the necessary control. (vv. 7–8)
4. Therefore, because of the danger that we will sin with our tongues, we should not teach others until our own lives demonstrate a godly consistency and spiritual maturity. (vv. 9–12)

First, James says, when someone is in control of his tongue, he can have a tremendously positive influence, he can accomplish great things. Small things, if they are under our control, can serve us well. Similarly, something as small as the tongue, if it's under control, can have a wonderful effect:

When we put bits into the mouths of horses to make them obey us, we can turn the whole animal. Or take ships as an example. Although they are so large and are driven by strong winds, they are steered by a very small rudder wherever the pilot wants to go. Likewise, the tongue is a small part of the body, but it makes great boasts. (2:3–5a)

Something very small, if controlled, can accomplish great things. Take a small thing like a bit in a horse's mouth—if the rider controls it, he can make the horse go any direction he wants. A huge ocean liner—blocks long, stories high—what gets it to its destination? A very small rudder under the control of the pilot's hand. What gets your car to parallel-park? Not your standing sideways and pushing it into the spot. No. What moves the huge car is something as small as a power-steering wheel that you control.

Little things, when you have control of them, can accomplish great results. So also the tongue, a little thing, a small part of the body, when controlled, can do much good.

- Think of Winston Churchill, with his words, holding the British people together during World War II.
- Think of a mother, with the right words, building the self-image of a child.
- Think of a teacher, with the appropriate comment, instilling confidence in a student.
- Think of a husband or wife, knowing exactly which words to say to comfort or encourage the other.

Something as little as the tongue can do much good—the power of a compliment, the protection of a warning ("Look out!"). When our tongues are in control, we can accomplish great good. On the other hand, when something small is not in control, it can cause unbelievable, irreparable damage. James says, "Consider what a great forest is set on fire by a small spark." A forest fire that destroys miles of timber and hundreds of homes, and claims the lives of animals, home-owners and firefighters—that great blazing, destroying, consuming inferno, was started by a small fire that wasn't controlled—a match, a cigarette tip, the flick of a lighter. Something small, not in control, can cause great damage. So too the tongue—it's small, but it too is a fire. "The tongue also is a fire, a world of evil." The world's evil, sinful way of handling stress is to abuse with the tongue. And the capacity of this tongue, this small part of the body, the capacity of this small tongue to hurt and destroy is beyond calculation—"it corrupts the whole body, sets the whole course of one's life on fire." It can start us down a path that we will forever regret—a word spoken to a spouse in anger becomes a memory in the marriage for years to come; an uncontrolled outburst humiliates a child, and the child for decades struggles to overcome a poor self-image; a thoughtless, cutting remark belittles a friend, and the rest of life is affected by it. The tongue "is itself set on fire by hell." Hell itself seems able to ignite the tongue to cause such damage and destruction. (3:5b–6)

When we are in control of our tongues, we can accomplish great things. But when we are not in control of our tongues, we can cause great damage. Unfortunately, the sad truth is—very few of us have this necessary control. We can control almost anything else, but it's so hard to get control of the tongue:

All kinds of animals, birds, reptiles and sea creatures are being tamed and have been tamed by mankind, but no human being can tame the tongue. It is a restless evil, full of deadly poison. (3:7–8)

We can tame and control everything in the animal world. We can tame animals—we can get tigers to jump through hoops, elephants to dance. We can tame birds—we have hunting falcons and homing pigeons. We can tame reptiles—a hooded cobra will sway out of a basket to the tunes of a flute. We can tame the sea creatures—go to Marine Land or Sea World and see the seals clapping, dolphins swimming in synchronization, whales carrying a rider.

We can tame and control everything in the animal world, but somehow the tongue resists control. It's restless, slippery, we can't pin it down. It slithers, and when it strikes, it's full of deadly poison. We do not have it in control.

Therefore, James concludes, in stressful situations when the actions of some are causing difficulties and trials for the rest of us, we should be very slow to step forward and "teach" others what they should do. It's too likely we won't be able to control our tongues, and will sin against them. Instead, we should first make sure our own lives demonstrate a godly consistency and spiritual maturity. As long as there is inconsistency in us and in our speech, as long as we don't have control of our tongues, we're in no position to tell others what to do.

With the tongue we praise our Lord and Father, and with it we curse human beings, who have been made in God's likeness. Out of the same mouth come praise and cursing. My brothers and sisters, this should not be. (3:9–10)

We praise God loudly during Sunday worship. But later, in the congregational business meeting, we ream out a fellow believer. Such an inconsistency ought not to occur. It certainly doesn't occur anywhere else in nature. "Can both fresh water and salt water flow from the same spring" (3:11)? Does an underground spring, bubbling up, one day give you fresh water and the next day bitter water? No. In nature, there's always a consistency; you always get the same thing.

Nature reveals the consistency God intends—where what is true in the heart always comes out. "My brothers and sisters, can a fig tree bear olives, or a grapevine bear figs?" No, a fig tree will consistently produce figs. A grapevine will consistently produce grapes. It's in their DNA—the essence deep inside always shows up on the outside. "Neither can a salt spring produce fresh water" (3:12).

The same needs to be true before anyone presumes to teach others how they should behave during difficult times. Let the teachers first demonstrate consistent godliness and maturity, so that we will know that deep inside all the areas of their lives are in control. Then we will trust that their tongues also will be in control when they rise to offer counsel to the rest of us.

This is James's caution: When the behavior of some is causing difficulties for others, "not many of you should become teachers." The chances are too great that you will sin. The only people who should teach others in such situations are those who are consistently in control of all areas of their lives.

8

WISE OR OTHERWISE

James 3:13–18

In one of the *Peanuts* comic strips, Lucy philosophizes to Charlie Brown: "Life is like a deck chair, Charlie Brown. Some place it so they can see where they are going; some place it so they can see where they have been; and some place it so they can see where they are at present." Charlie Brown listens, and then replies, "I can't even get mine unfolded."

There are times when we all feel like that—we need help with our deck chairs. How can we get life unfolded so that we can settle into it? Who can help us? Who has the wisdom or insight to point us in the right direction?

When we were younger and thought our parents knew everything, we turned to them for advice. But sometimes even they were no help. Andy Rooney, the wry commentator on TV's *60 Minutes* for many years, regrets the advice he forgot to give his kids before they left home:[*]

- Throw away the can of paint after you've finished painting something, no matter how much there is left in the can.
- Go to bed. Whatever you're staying up late for isn't worth it.
- Nothing important is ever said in a phone conversation that lasts more than three minutes.
- Don't do your Christmas shopping too early. It isn't as much fun.
- In a conversation, keep in mind that you're more interested in what you have to say than anyone else is.

---

[*] *The Dallas Times Herald*, November 17, 1983.

- Money shouldn't be saved for a rainy day. It should be saved and spent for a beautiful day.
- When you cross a street, look both ways even on a one-way street.

Sometimes we're stepping into one of life's streets without fully knowing the dangers. We don't know what to expect, which way to look, which direction to go. Who can help us? Whom should we listen to?

If we're having difficulty with one of our small children, which woman in the mother's club should we take advice from? If our marriage is going through a rocky spell, which guy on the softball team should we talk to about it? If we're among our friends, talking about which colleges to go to, what to major in, and which courses to take, whose opinion should matter to us? If we're discussing the youth ministry at church—whether to focus on small groups and discipleship or to plan large scale events to draw unchurched teens—whose thoughts should matter to us? In situations of differing opinions, disagreements, and potential conflict, whom should we listen to? Who will have God's wisdom? Out of all the counsel and advice available, who will be right?

In the early years of Christianity, a group of Christians needed to know the answer to that question. As a group, they were facing external pressures and persecutions. Different members of their group were offering advice—often heatedly and insistently, convinced they were right. Were they? Others had different views. Whom should these believers to listen to?

James, their former pastor wrote them, "Don't listen to the person who too quickly steps forward to instruct the group. Very likely that person won't have control of his tongue, and whatever of the world's evil that is in that person will come out, and his words will offend others sinfully. Watch out for the person who too quickly presumes to teach others regarding a difficult situation. Don't listen to that person" (paraphrased from 3:1–12).

Then whom should we listen to? To whom should we should look for guidance? How can we recognize the one who will have God's wisdom in the matter? That's the questions James now raises:

Who is wise and understanding among you? (3:13a)

To be wise and understanding meant to know both where to go and how to get there, to know which direction was right and what specific steps should be taken to get to the destination. To be wise was to know the goal God wanted; to be understanding was to know how to reach it. How can we recognize such a person?

James first gives a summary answer to this question and then develops his answer in more detail. His summary answer is in verse 13, and his more detailed explanation is in verses 14–18.

James's summary answer as to how we can spot one who is wise and understanding is: Look for the gentle and humble person whose life you admire. Look for the person who just quietly goes about doing good.

> *Who is wise and understanding among you? Let them show it by their good life, by deeds done in the humility that comes from wisdom.* (3:13)

Wise and understanding people will be marked by gentle *humility*. They will be quietly at ease with themselves. They won't act like they have the answer to every question. They won't be too quick to make speeches or offer solutions. Nor will they seem to be ego-driven on the matter, as though they had something to prove. Further, you'll be impressed with the good lives of wise people. You'll admire their quiet tangible deeds done on behalf of others.

When you see this combination—of deeds done in humility—you can be confident that such a person's counsel comes from wisdom. This is the person who will have God's truth for your situation. This is the person to whom you should listen.

James then expands on this summary answer. He first explains more fully whom we should not listen to (vv. 14–16) and then describes more specifically the godly qualities of the person we should listen to (vv. 17–18).

We should not listen to the person who is lacking in humility, who seems to be ego-involved in the situation:

> *But if you harbor bitter envy and selfish ambition in your hearts, do not boast about it or deny the truth. Such "wisdom" does not come down from heaven but is earthly, unspiritual, demonic. For where you have*

envy and selfish ambition, there you find disorder and every evil practice. (3:14–16)

We can usually spot such ego-involvement in two ways—the person will harbor bitter envy and have a selfish ambition. Such people are envious of us and others. Their own lives have not been successful: their children have not turned out well; their marriages have not flourished; they didn't attend the school they wanted, or achieve the grades they needed. And out of this bitter envy, people are quick to give advice which justifies themselves—shifting the blame for their failures onto others.

Their ego-involvement also shows in their selfish ambition—they seem to be after some underlying personal gain or prestige through their advice. They want prominence, attention. Or they want to brag to others that they had influence with us. Or they're playing to some audience that can help them with some agenda or project or event. This selfish ambition leads people to be stubborn and insistent, attempting to press their opinions on others. To them, it's more important to gain followers than to find God's guidance, to win the argument than to be right. They're after a victory more than they are after truth. Such people cannot claim to have God's wisdom for the situation. Whatever advice they give "does not come down from heaven, but is instead earthly, unspiritual, demonic."

In a congregation, a bitterly envious and selfishly ambitious person will only raise the decibel level and produce disorder in the church—unrest, turmoil, agitation, polarization, disharmony. And the result will be "every evil practice" among the members—backbiting, angry accusations, taking sides, setting up cliques, judging others. Do not listen to such a person. Instead, listen to the gentle, humble person whose motives are pure and whose words continually produce peace within the congregation. Listen to the person who has nothing to prove, nothing to gain, whose life demonstrates the fruit of the Spirit, and whose every action leaves peace lingering in the air:

> *But the wisdom that comes from heaven is first of all pure; then peace-*
> *loving, considerate, submissive, full of mercy and good fruit, impartial*

and sincere. Peacemakers who sow in peace reap a harvest of righteousness. (3:17–18)

People who have "the wisdom that comes from heaven" will first of all be pure—having no ego involvement in the situation, no agenda, no ulterior motives. Because they themselves are peace-loving, they always bring peace to a tense situation, either by being considerate when they are in the dominant position in a relationship, or by being submissive when they are in the subordinate position. Being considerate, they overlook small faults and give others credit for their character over the long haul. Being submissive, they are not difficult to lead or persuade, but quietly and easily join in with others. Their whole life is "full of mercy and good fruit"—spent generously helping those in need and practically serving the interests others. You know such people will be impartial, not choosing nor favoring one side or person over another, and sincere, not flattering or pretending in order to gain some benefit.

When you want to know God's wisdom for a situation, whether personally or in a church, listen to the gentle, humble people whose words bring peace, for theirs is the counsel that will lead to success—to "a harvest of righteousness."

9

HE GIVES MORE GRACE

James 4:1–6

After I graduated from college I moved to Dallas to begin seminary studies. In the very first week of class at the seminary I took an instant dislike to a fellow first-year student. Why?

We had never met each other before—he was from Pennsylvania, I was from California. There had been no conversations between us to that point; his last name was at the beginning of the alphabet, mine was at the end, so we were never next to each other in any seating or line. We seldom saw each other outside of class; he was married, living off campus; I was single, living on campus in men's housing. Yet, out of the 100–150 students who started in that freshman class, within one week, I took an intense dislike to him. Why?

At the same time that I was going to seminary, I also had a part-time job at a Dallas newspaper. My hours were from six to ten in the evening. My job was dismantling and setting up the large ads that appeared daily in the paper. This was in the day when the outside borders of each ad were formed with pre-cast metal strips giving the stores' names, addresses, logos, and other such boilerplate information. The internal copy of the ads was prepared elsewhere. My first task on arriving was to peel the tape from the ads that had run that day and file the strips and logos in appropriate drawers. Finishing that, I then went back to the drawers and found the necessary materials to create the next day's ads.

I was often able to complete all my work before ten o'clock. And my boss that first year let me go home as soon as I finished, even though the company would pay me for the full four hours I had been scheduled to work. Since I usually had lots of homework, I was very appreciative. The boss was a great guy; we got along fine.

When summer came, I returned to California to work and get married. During my absence from the newspaper, my boss got promoted, and one of my fellow workers, who was full-time, took his place. As fellow workers, we too had gotten along just great. But when I returned for my second year of work at the paper, and he was now my boss, things changed. There was constant tension and bickering and shortness between us. I had a sub-surface anger toward him for months. Why?

What causes us to be angry, to fight, to have quarrels?

Think about your relationships right now. Who are you angry with and why? Who are you upset with, ticked-off at, resentful of? Why? In your family—with your spouse, children, parents, siblings—who do you find yourself bickering and quarreling with? Why? When you gather with your relatives, where is the tension? At school, who are the students or teachers that make you mad? At the company you work for, in the office you go to, who do you dislike and try to have the least contact with? In the business you're involved with, who's the competitor you're angry with? In the group you belong to—whether PTA, Junior League, booster club, task force, planning committee, sports club, Sunday school class, or church—who are you irritated with? Why?

What causes us to be angry, to fight, to quarrel, to hope someone gets taken down a peg or two? What causes us to feel this way?

Our obvious answer, as we think of the person or situation, is because "he did this or that" or "she does such and such." We're angry, or dislike people, because of some action on their part.

The reason I disliked my fellow classmate at seminary was because he sat in the front row of every class, right in front of the professor, and agreed with everything the professor said in a vigorous, verbal way—"Oh, yes, praise God." "Oh, that's terrible. Tsk."—accompanied by either a definite nod or shake of his head. My reaction was, "What a kiss-up!" That's why I disliked him.

The reason I disliked the fellow worker who had become my boss the second year at the newspaper was because he used his new authority to be petty and mean toward me, to rub my face in his new superiority over me. My job paid minimum wage for the four hours each night I worked. If I hurried and finished early, there was no reason why I couldn't go home, while still being paid for the full four hours. This made the low hourly wage more "respectable" to me. Most nights I could leave shortly after eight o'clock. Some nights, everything would be done except for one ad that was still being prepared for the next day and would not be ready for me until near the end of my shift. My boss the first year always said, "Go home. No use you hanging around with nothing to do just for one ad. I have to stay here anyway. If they send the ad up, I'll get the strips and logos it needs." So I would leave, grateful for the extra two hours of study.

The fellow worker who became my boss the second year was several years younger than me. I was in graduate school; he was a year or two out of high school. And for some reason, he enjoyed letting me know that he was my boss and in control. When I asked for his permission to leave, having finished my work, he would say, "No, there's another ad coming in, and you have to stay here to process it." And I would have to hang around for an hour or two for just one ad, which he could have taken care of for me. That's why I disliked him—because he used his petty authority to be mean to me.

That's our obvious answer as to why we are angry or resentful or quarreling—because of some action on someone else's part, something that person does or did.

But as James writes to his former church members about the tensions and conflicts they're having with each other as they experience trials and difficulties in their new cities, he says that the reasons for our resentments and quarrels with each other are much more profound and penetrating than, "This is what they've done," or "This is what they're like." He says that if we find ourselves disliking other believers, being angry with them and hoping they'll get taken down a peg or two, the reasons are not in the other people—the reasons are in us. And if we're going to come through our trials to the righteousness, completeness, maturity, and crown of life that God has in mind, we must understand what is really at the heart of our conflicts with others.

What causes our fights, and what can be done about it? These are the questions James asks, and answers.

"What causes fights and quarrels among you?" he asks (4:1a). The reasons, he says, are in us, and there are two.

The first reason we are ready to fight and quarrel is because our own desires are being denied. There's something we want, and we aren't getting it. This other person is either getting it instead or is stopping us from getting it. Our desires, our wants, are being frustrated, thwarted, denied, and we see the other person as responsible. So we're angry, resentful, ready to fight, hoping he or she will get what we think is coming to them:

> What causes fights and quarrels among you? Don't they come from your desires that battle within you? You desire but do not have, so you kill. You covet but you cannot get what you want, so you quarrel and fight. (4:1–2a)

The cause of our fights and quarrels is some self-centered desire that wants to prevail. There is some "me, my, mine" that is being insisted on.

The desires that James has in mind are not some innocent pleasures, as in our idiom, "What's your desire?" It's not something innocuous, such as, "What would you like? What do you want? What would please you?" These are insistent, belligerent desires. They're ready to wage war; they battle within us. James's image is a military one—armed soldiers getting into battle formation, ready to go out in a bitter campaign to get what they want. We have an innate, self-centered readiness to fight to get our own way. We desire and covet—wanting something someone else has, but we do not have it and cannot get it. So we're ready to kill and destroy, to quarrel and fight with those who are keeping it from us.

Why did I dislike my fellow seminary student? Because I wanted to be noticed by the professors. I wanted to make a favorable impression on them. I was entering the first phase of my ministry career, and I wanted them to say about me, "Sunukjian, you've got what it takes." Instead, this other student was making a good impression instead of me.

Could that be the cause of your resentment of someone—you want to be admired, esteemed, accepted, honored, but the other person is getting it instead of you? Someone else at school is getting the popularity you want? Someone in your group is gaining the leadership or influence you want?

Someone at work is picked for the promotion or raise you want? Someone else is getting the date you want to attract? Could the reason for your animosity be because "you desire but do not have, you covet but you cannot get what you want"?

Why was I upset with my boss the second year at the newspaper? Because I wanted to go home early and study. Because I considered myself better than a minimum-wage worker, and getting paid for four hours while only working two helped soothe my ego. Because I wanted to be in control of my schedule rather than him.

Could that be the reason for your tension with someone—a desire to control, a resentment over someone else's control? Your husband controls the hours he puts in on the job, not you. Your parents control your curfew, your groundings, who your friends are and what you do with them. Your longtime friend controls the relationship, always wanting to do things a certain way.

Could the reason for bad-mouthing a competitor be due to a desire for success—he's having it and you're not? His numbers are up; yours are down. His share of the market, his sales volume, his client base is increasing; yours are decreasing. He's getting the reputation in the field; you're not.

Could the reason for resenting a fellow worker be due to the success she's having instead of you? She got picked for the sales trip to Paris. She's being spoken of as a comer, a producer for the company.

When our desires are denied or thwarted, our response is to quarrel and fight. These are violent words—they imply a smoldering state of hostility which repeatedly flares into an outburst of antagonism; an enduring feud with recurring bouts of conflict. We're even ready to kill, as James says—to harm whomever we think is responsible, to wish him or her gone from the picture. We want to destroy the rival or obstacle that interferes with our desire. We're close to thinking, "I wish you were dead, out of here! I hope you get yours!"

That's the first reason, James says, why we're angry and wish another ill—because our own desires are being denied. We want, but aren't getting. So we're ready to attack and battle and beat the one who stands in our way.

There's a second reason, James says, why we find ourselves inclined to fight and quarrel: because we have stopped trusting God to be good to us.

We no longer believe that he is planning good for our life and is able to give us every good thing. We're starting to accuse him: "You won't give it to me. You can't give it to me. You don't want to give it to me." We have to fight for it ourselves, because we have ceased depending on him as the one who can and will provide:

> *You do not have because you do not ask God. When you ask, you do not receive, because you ask with wrong motives, that you may spend what you get on your pleasures.* (4:2b–3)

We fail to pray because we do not really believe in God's ability or willingness to provide. We think he must have a limited supply, with not enough to go around, and if he gives it to another he won't have any for us. If my fellow student gains favor from the seminary professors, then I won't be able to get any.

Or it may be that God plays favorites. He'll give someone else an attractive person to date, but he won't do the same for me. We have ceased believing that God's riches and love are infinite and inexhaustible—beyond imagination.

If we do ask God for the thing we desire, we often ask with wrong motives. Our prayer is not guided by an honest seeking: "Is this something you want me to have? Will this be good for me? Do you have in mind another time and another way in which my heart's desires will be satisfied?" Instead, our prayer is an implicit selfish demand: "This is my agenda; now bless it, put your power to it. These are my goals; now make them happen. These are my pleasures, the things I want; now give them to me."

As we turn from a belief in God's goodness, as we abandon him because we no longer trust him, we end up embracing the world. We enter into a friendship with the world, believing instead that the world's methods are the ones to live by: "Look out for number one. Claw your way to the top. Win by intimidation. Be assertive. Don't take any guff." And so we quarrel and fight to get what we want.

James concludes with words drawn from the language of love and politics:

You adulterous people, don't you know that friendship with the world means enmity against God? Therefore, anyone who chooses to be a friend of the world becomes an enemy of God. (4:4)

We have become adulterous. We are the bride of Christ, but we have gone into the arms of another. We have turned from the intimacy and affection and care that our husband wants to lavish on us. We have said to him, "You're not adequate, you aren't satisfying me. What you're giving me is not enough. I'm going to get it elsewhere."

We have now become an enemy of God—there is hostility between us, as between two countries at war. The bond of peace has been repudiated; the relationship has been broken. We've gone back to an old alliance, to our former affiliation. Faced with pressures and trials, we've adopted the world's way of handling them—lashing out at fellow believers, quarreling and fighting with them because they are supposedly thwarting our desires, failing to bring the matter before God, and instead aligning ourselves once again with a sinful culture's way of doing things.

What is the cure? What is the answer to our adulterous tendency? What hope can we have to somehow rekindle our love and recapture our relationship with God?

Our hope lies in God's unshakable commitment to keep us intimate with him, and in the overwhelming grace he provides to make that happen. God is a jealous lover who simply will not let us go, and he will enable us to stay close to him:

Or do you think Scripture says without reason that he jealously longs for the spirit he has caused to dwell in us? But he gives us more grace. That is why Scripture says:

"God opposes the proud
but shows favor to the humble." (4:5–6)

God's response to our abandonment and our tendency to embrace the world is not rejection, but rather a fresh infusion of even more and greater grace to keep us connected to him. He will not let us remain in a hostile relationship with him, but instead will jealously woo back the spirit he put within us—a spirit that was created to have relationship and intimacy with him.

If necessary, he will use the negative pressure of opposing us if we continue our prideful behavior and our drift into the world's arms. But at the same time, he will give increasing grace if we turn in humble submission to him, accepting that our circumstances are difficult for the time being, but believing that he is working through them for good in our lives.

The grace or favor that God gives is not simply a benign aura, but rather an enabling power. It's a strengthening that enables us to move in a forward direction, just as his opposing the proud moves them in a backward direction. The Old Testament source of James's quote makes it clear that God is actively repelling the proud and advancing the humble; he is cursing the one and blessing the other:

> The LORD's curse is on the house of the wicked,
>   but he blesses the home of the righteous.
> He mocks proud mockers
>   but shows favor to the humble and oppressed.
> (Prov. 3:33–34)

After a couple of months of frustrating work with my second-year boss, one night he confided to me that his new wife was hitting the bars while he was working evenings at the paper. He also suspected her of infidelity. My heart went out to him. A couple of nights later he asked if I would drive him through an area of town when I got off work, so that he could see if his wife had driven their car to one of the bars. For an hour or two we slowly traversed the streets, returning several times to the same areas, to see if the car would show up, but without success. When I eventually returned him to the newspaper, I was no longer frustrated with his behavior. My desire to get home early seemed insignificant compared to his pain. From then on, we worked together in peace.

Praise God for his conquering grace.

10

NOT THY WILL BUT MINE BE DONE

James 4:7–12

The first sin in God's universe was someone saying, "Not thy will, but mine be done." Before God created our planet, before the human race appeared, before Eve contemplated a piece of fruit, someone in the highest court of heaven said, "Not thy will, but mine be done."

That was the sin of Lucifer—the highest angel God created, the one Scripture describes as the model of perfection, full of wisdom beyond all other angels, dazzlingly perfect in beauty. Over time, as he dwelt in the splendor of heaven, pride rose in his heart, and he said, "I will raise my throne above the stars of God. I will make myself like the Most High. I will run heaven and be worshipped. Things will be the way I want them. I will be God" (see Isa. 14:12–14; Ezek. 28:11–17). Through this sin of pride, he set himself against God, becoming an enemy of God. And God cast him out of heaven.

But his rebellion against God continued, and he was eventually able to convince the first humans on earth to repeat his sin—to assert their will against God's. "Do what you want," he hissed to Eve, "not what God wants. God's holding back something good from you, something that will make you equal with him. He doesn't want you to have it. But you don't have to put up with that. If you really want it, you can have it. Don't let God decide. You decide."

And out of Eve's heart came the same thought, "Not thy will, but mine be done. Not the way you want it, but the way I want it." And Adam agreed.

Through this sin of pride, they set themselves against God, becoming enemies of God. And God cast them out of Eden.

Satan's rebellion continues today. In his bitter hatred of God and his desire to wreak havoc, Satan comes to each one of us and hisses similar thoughts to us—"It doesn't look like God's going to give you what you want. It looks like he's going to let things stay the way you don't want them to be. But that doesn't have to be the case. You don't have to put up with that. It doesn't have to be what God wants. It can be what you want."

Or, "It looks like you've gone as high as you're going to go in this company you work for. That promotion you were hoping for—it looks like they've got their eye on someone else for the job instead of you. Is God being good to you? If this is what he wants, it's certainly not what you want, is it? But you don't have to settle for this. You have options. You can quit. You can go work for a competitor and help them surge ahead of this company. That would show these people, wouldn't it? Or maybe you can still get the promotion in this company—bad-mouth the guy they have their eye on, drop comments that cause others to think less of him. Be careful, of course, not to be too obvious as you point out his shortcomings. Maybe you can still swing things your way. What do you want? Don't let God decide. You decide."

Or, "It doesn't look like God's going to give you the kind of marriage you want. Your spouse hasn't changed, things haven't gotten better, and she doesn't seem to care. Apparently you're not important to her; it doesn't seem to matter to her how you feel about it. But you don't have to put up with that. You have options. Two can play at that game. You know how to hurt her too. You can make her life miserable in return. Or you can leave, quit, bail out on the marriage. Surely there's someone at the office, or in the neighborhood, or on the Internet who can provide the affection, admiration, and laughter you're not getting at home. What kind of marriage do you want? You don't have to let God decide. You decide."

Or, "If God's not going to give you what you want, why should you give him the devotion he wants? If he's not going to give you the boyfriend or girlfriend you want to date, the school you want to attend, the neighborhood you want to live in, the retirement income you want to live on, why should you give him the obedience, worship, and service he asks for? You've got options. You can bail out, live life without him, go your own way."

This is the voice of Satan. And if Satan convinces us to raise ourselves against God, we will make ourselves an enemy that God will have to oppose. But God woos us jealously, asking us to trust him and standing ready to bless us if we will humble ourselves before him (4:4–6).

It's on this note that James concludes his discussion of the world's first way of coping with trials—lashing out against others, fighting and quarreling with them because they seem to be aggravating our difficulties, demanding that they act the way we want them to act, with our only prayer being, "God, make everything be the way I want it to be."

In contrast to the world's way of reacting, James instead now appeals to us to submit to what God is doing in our lives, to accept that things will be difficult for a while, and to not sit in judgment of others. Rather than demanding that things be done to suit us, either in our personal lives or in the church, we should accept our circumstances as sorrowful for the time being. And as we submit to how God has fashioned things, he will eventually lift us up:

> Submit yourselves, then, to God. Resist the devil, and he will flee from you. Come near to God and he will come near to you. Wash your hands, you sinners, and purify your hearts, you double-minded. Grieve, mourn and wail. Change your laughter to mourning and your joy to gloom. Humble yourselves before the Lord, and he will lift you up.
>
> Brothers and sisters, do not slander one another. Anyone who speaks against a brother or sister or judges them speaks against the law and judges it. When you judge the law, you are not keeping it, but sitting in judgment on it. There is only one Lawgiver and Judge, the one who is able to save and destroy. But you—who are you to judge your neighbor? (4:7–12)

Verses 7a and 10 are parallel statements: "Submit yourselves, then, to God," and "Humble yourselves before the Lord." The verses in between (vv. 7b–9) describe what this humble submitting would look like as far as

God is concerned, and the verses which follow (vv.10–12) describe what it would look like as far as other believers are concerned.

To submit humbly to what God is doing through our trials means first that we will resist the devil. Instead of giving an ear to his insinuation that "God is not being good to you," we will affirm in faith, "The Lord is good. He is the giver of every good and perfect gift (1:17). He only does good in my life." Instead of letting Satan turn us away from God, we will come near to God, and we will sense him coming near to us.

As we resist the devil, and as we and God lovingly draw near to each other, Satan will actually *flee* from us. He won't just leave us alone; he'll do whatever he can to distance himself from us rapidly. This is because he knows that our humble submission to God is a grave threat to him and his own evil kingdom. God is about to lift us up, and his power is about to work through us. And Satan flees in fear. As C. S. Lewis has Screwtape, a senior demon, explain to his underling Wormwood:

> Our cause is never more in danger than when a human being, no longer desiring, but still intending, to do our Enemy's will, looks round upon a universe from which every trace of Him seems to have vanished, and asks why he has been forsaken, and still obeys.[*]

To submit humbly means that we will wash our hands of sin and purify our hearts and cease being double-minded about whether God is in our trials for good. James is echoing his opening comments about our need to "get rid of all moral filth and the evil that is so prevalent" (1:14–15; 21), and our need to believe and not doubt that God is working good in us, lest we be unstable in our double-mindedness (1:6–7).

In our submission, we may grieve and mourn for the heaviness of our trials. We may wail over our failures or lapses during them. We can accept that our circumstances do not presently elicit laughter and joy. But our conviction is secure: the Lord is good, and he will eventually lift us up.

As we submit humbly before God, we then become gentle and kind toward others. We do not slander them or judge them for how their actions have affected us. That would be a violation of the law of love, and the

---

[*] C. S. Lewis, *The Screwtape Letters* (New York: Macmillan, 1961), 39.

Lawgiver would then sit in judgment of us. Instead, our actions toward others become peace-loving, considerate, submissive, and full of mercy (3:17). Again, James is echoing some earlier comments as he wraps up his plea that we avoid being polluted by the world's way of responding to trials by blaming others (1:27; 2:8–13; 3:1–4:10).

As we submit humbly to what God is doing, and as he hears from us what he heard from his Son—"Not my will, but yours be done" (Luke 22:42)— our lives become filled with peace and joy.

11

DON'T LEAVE HOME WITHOUT IT

James 4:13–17

Nell and I were living in Dallas the day John F. Kennedy was shot. I was in graduate school at the time. I have three vivid memories from that day.

First, I remember where I was when I first heard the news. They say that's very common for people—to remember exactly where they were when they heard something momentous. I was outside the school library, talking with a friend, when another student came up to tell us the news.

My second memory: I remember the route Kennedy's motorcade was on when the shooting occurred. I went that same route every day on my way to my part-time job with the freight lines. I knew the curve of the road. I knew the rise of the grassy knoll. I knew the Texas School Depository Building overlooking the street.

My most vivid memory, though, is the third one. I remember the evening of the shooting. I was watching the TV footage that had been filmed just eight hours earlier that day—the motorcade moving through the streets of Dallas, Kennedy in the open car, smiling, waving, pointing, laughing, not knowing that in the next few minutes his life would end. And as I looked at the man on the screen who had been smiling, alive, I found myself thinking, "You have no idea that in a few minutes you will die."

There was an item in our newspaper not too long ago about a thirty-four year old man down at the beach, splashing in three feet of water with a friend. Suddenly a rip tide took him out beyond his depth, and despite being rescued and receiving mouth-to-mouth resuscitation, he was pronounced dead within an hour.

Also in our newspaper: a man and wife in their fifties, on a motorcycle, were approaching the toll booth to get a ticket to enter the toll road. A driver in the next lane suddenly realized he didn't want to go onto the toll road, and made a U-turn, not seeing the motorcycle coming up. The husband suffered moderate injuries, but the wife's injuries were fatal, and she died three days later.

On the television news, we see a car driving safely down the street, another car running a red light, a crash, and the passenger in the first car dies.

Common to all of these events is the sheer unexpectedness of what happened. The people involved had no idea it was coming. Kennedy, the man splashing in three feet of water, the man and wife on a motorcycle, the passenger in the car—it was the furthest thing from their minds. They didn't expect it to happen.

None of us, as we sit here, expect anything like this to happen to us. Neither did they. But the honest truth is, we don't really know what will happen the rest of today, or tomorrow, or this week, or in the next few months.

And because this is true—that we don't really know what's ahead—the Scriptures say it ought to affect how we plan, how we set out on the days that are ahead. The fact that we don't know what's coming, the Bible says, ought to affect our thoughts about the future—not to make us morbidly preoccupied with fears of looming disasters, nor to fill us with gloom or anxiety. But instead, in very practical ways, it ought to affect how we schedule things on our calendars.

Because you don't know what is coming, there is a certain way you ought not to plan, and a certain way you should plan. Because you don't know for sure what's ahead, there's something you should avoid in your planning, and something you should include in your planning.

Are you making plans for school next semester? What classes you will take. What major you will have. Where you will live. What part-time work you will do. What year you will graduate. What you will do when you get out of school. Are you making those plans?

Are you making plans for marriage? How long you will be engaged. What date the wedding will be. Where it will be held. What kind of reception you will have. How many attendants will be in the bridal party. What color the dresses will be. Where you will honeymoon. The first place you will live as a couple. Are you planning those things?

Are you making plans for your company or your career? The goals you will focus on for the next year. The new products or services you will offer. The new territories or markets you will enter. The equipment or certification you will need.

Are you making plans for your vacation this summer? Planning what day you will leave. Where you will go. How you will get there. How long you will stay. What you will do while there. How much you will spend. Whom you will see. When you will return. Are you planning those things?

Are you making plans for your retirement? How many more years you will work. What funds you will have available. What age you will start drawing Social Security or taking from your IRA. What you will do during retirement. Where you will live. Are some of these things in the planning stage?

As you think about all these things that are in the future, there's a certain way, James says, that you ought not to plan, and a certain way you should plan. There's something you should avoid in your planning, and something you should include in your planning.

James is writing to his former church members who are going through difficult trials. He's urged them to look for God's good purposes in the trials (1:1-25), to love each other impartially and tangibly during the trials (2:1-26), and to keep themselves from being polluted by the world's way of handling trials. One way those in the world react to trials is by lashing out against others, fighting and quarreling with those they think are aggravating the difficulties, and demanding that they change their ways. Our response instead, James says, should be to submit to what God is doing in our lives, accept that things will be difficult for a while, and wait for God to lift us up (3:1–4:12).

But those in the world have a second way of trying to cope with trials: they try to protect themselves from the trial by planning to get rich. They focus their thoughts and energies on gaining wealth as a means of insulating themselves from the trial.

James now addresses this second polluting response, first by focusing on the arrogance of thinking that we can plan anything confidently

(4:13–17), and then by exposing the all-too-common sins of the rich that bring God's judgment on them (5:1–6). His identical opening words—"Now listen"—and his repeated references to money and wealth tie these two units together. We'll first consider the foolishness of thinking we can plan anything with confidence, and then in the next chapter we'll look at the sinful tendencies that come with being rich, tendencies that can too easily move us from the frying pan of "trials" into the fire of "judgment." Because we don't know for sure what's ahead, there's a certain way we ought not to plan, and a certain way we should plan.

How ought we not to plan? What should we avoid in our planning?

First, James says, we ought not to plan with any sense of finality or certainty, as though we control the future. We should avoid any thought of saying, "This is it. I've nailed it down. This is what I'm going to do."

> Now listen, you who say, "Today or tomorrow we will go to this or that city, spend a year there, carry on business and make money." Why, you do not even know what will happen tomorrow. What is your life? You are a mist that appears for a little while and then vanishes. Instead, you ought to say, "If it is the Lord's will, we will live and do this or that." As it is, you boast in your arrogant schemes. All such boasting is evil. If anyone, then, knows the good they ought to do and doesn't do it, it is sin for them. (4:13–17)*

Verse 13 describes a group of businessmen. They're traders. They have goods, products, to sell. They see that they can do better in another location—there's a better market in another city, where they can get higher prices. "We will go to this or that city, spend a year there, carry on business and make money." So they set a departure date—"today or tomorrow we

---

* James 4:13–16 is a *chiasm*—the sequential top and bottom units match each other and the middle point of the structure indicates the main emphasis:

A   Arrogantly planning your future is evil (4:13).
  B   You do not know what you will do (4:14a),
    C   Or even whether you will live (4:14b).
      D   It's up to the Lord (4:15a)
    C   Whether you will live (4:15b),
  B   And what you will do (4:15c).
A   Arrogantly planning your future is evil (4:16).

will go to this or that city"; and they plan how long they will stay—we will "spend a year there."

They're businessmen with a one-year plan—company executives, manufacturers' representatives, investment bankers. They've set goals. They know the profit margin they want. They've got the networks; they know whom to contact. They're going in at the ground floor. Get in early and get out fast. Hold for a year, sell for a profit. Life is set. This is the plan. Sell it to the stockholders.

Now don't misunderstand. The Bible is not against our making plans. On the contrary, the Bible encourages us to plan. We should think about the future, and plan wisely for it. Take a lesson from the ant, the Bible says. It plans ahead for the future:

> Go to the ant, you sluggard;
> > consider its ways and be wise!
> It has no commander,
> > no overseer or ruler,
> yet it stores its provisions in summer
> > and gathers its food at harvest. (Prov. 6:6–8)

The ant gathers and stores up when things are plentiful—during summer and harvest—because it knows there will be long months of winter when little is available. It sets something aside for a later time. It saves for the future. You too should plan now for what you will need in the future.

The Bible recognizes the benefits of careful, diligent planning: "The plans of the diligent lead to profit as surely as haste leads to poverty" (Prov. 21:5). Good plans lead to good results—a profit. Rushing hastily forward, without a plan, leads to disaster. It's like our American adage: "If we fail to plan, we plan to fail."

We should plan. The issue is not whether we should plan, but how we should plan, the way we should plan.

The wrong way to plan, James says, is with a sense of finality and certainty, as though you're in control of what will happen. "Here's what I'm going to do. Here's how I'm going to do it. And this is going to be the result."

Planning that way, James says, is arrogant and evil: "As it is, you boast in your arrogant schemes. All such boasting is evil" (4:16). It is to plan with the assumption that "Everything's set. All my ducks are in order. I've got it all planned." It's to plan with a sense of finality and certainty, as though now you're in control of what will happen. That attitude, James says, is arrogant and evil.

Why is such planning arrogant? Why is it wrong to have the attitude: "This is the plan, all my ducks are in order, and everything's set"?

Because of three reasons, James says. First, it's arrogant because you don't know what will happen tomorrow. You don't know what the future is going to be.

You plan, tomorrow, to go to work. That's what you plan. And probably that will happen. But you don't know for sure what your life will be like tomorrow. Your alarm may not go off, and you could be an hour late in getting started. That delay may get you trapped on the freeway for hours because of an accident that blocks all three lanes for six hours. You plan, but you can't control for sure what will happen.

You plan, tomorrow, to take your children to school. That will probably happen, but you don't know for sure. The child may wake up sick. Your car may have a dead battery. We don't really know what will happen tomorrow, or this week, or next month.

What am I planning for tomorrow? I plan to start teaching a three-week intensive course at the seminary. We'll meet every day for three weeks, from nine to noon. The material for handouts is already prepared and sitting on my desk. I know which set I'll distribute on Monday, then a new set on Tuesday, none on Wednesday, then a third set on Thursday. I've planned the sequence. I know how much I need to cover each day in order to get everything in.

I've got my plans. But I don't really know what will happen tomorrow. I could wake up with a throat infection, lose my voice, have laryngitis—and not be able to say a word. Or I could get to campus and find a bomb scare that means we have to evacuate the school. Or, I could start teaching at nine, and at ten have a spasm in my neck which would make it impossible to go on.

I don't really know what will happen this week or month from now. What am I planning for a month from now? A month from now Nell and I will fly to New York for a weekend conference of Chinese pastors and educators from the Northeast. They've asked me to be their conference speaker. In addition to speaking, Nell and I will each present a three-hour seminar at the conference—mine will be on preaching, hers will be on women's ministries. I'll follow on Sunday by preaching twice in a local church, and then from Monday through Thursday, with the help of a translator, I'll teach a course in a Chinese seminary, covering two New Testament books.

That's what Nell and I are going to do. Maybe. But maybe they'll cancel the weekend conference because too few people register for it due to economic cutbacks. Or maybe a snowstorm will cancel all flights into the New York airport. Or maybe American Airlines will go on strike.

You don't really know what will happen tomorrow, or this week, or next month, or this year.

What are you planning for this year, for your company, your career? What could change those plans? Could the company be bought out? Could new technology make the company obsolete? Could a competitor come out with something better, cheaper? Could Congress pass laws that would hurt your operations or profits? Could a rival company offer you incentives to switch jobs? You really don't know what your life will be like tomorrow.

Is your life today like what you thought it would be three years ago? Or have there been some unexpected turns in the last three years? How much notice did you have before the unexpected turn happened? How many months in advance did you know it would happen? Zip. Nada. Is it possible another unexpected turn is ahead of you, in the next two or three months, and that right now you have zero notice of it?

That's the first reason, James says, why it's arrogant to plan with a sense of finality and certainty—"You do not even know what will happen tomorrow" (4:14a.).

The second reason it's arrogant to plan with a sense of certainty is because, not only do you not know what the future will be like, you don't know for certain that you will be here for the future. Not only are you unable to control tomorrow, but you don't even know for sure you'll be around tomorrow. Your planning is arrogant because you don't really know how long you have to live. "What is your life? You are a mist that appears for a little while and then vanishes" (4:14b).

To plan confidently as though you know "this is what's going to happen" is arrogant, James says, because you don't know how long you have to live. You know how long your past has been, but you don't know how long your future will be. Your life is a mist, a wisp of smoke that is here briefly, and then gone. As though one strikes a match, and the vapor dissipates into the air. That's how permanent your life is. That's how much you can count on being around. You're here, you're gone.

If I asked you, "Do you expect to die?" you would say, "Yes." If I asked you, "Do you expect to die by Wednesday?" you would say, "No." But of all the people in the country who are going to die between now and Wednesday, how many, right now, are expecting it to happen?

It's arrogant, James says, to plan with a sense of finality and certainty—"This is it. This is what I'm going to do." You do not know what will happen tomorrow, and you do not know if you will even be here tomorrow.

There's a third reason, James gives us why such planning is not only arrogant, but also actually evil: "As it is, you boast in your arrogant schemes. All such boasting is evil" (4:16). And the reason it's evil is because we act as though a sovereign controlling God doesn't exist. To have the attitude that "This is the plan. This is what I'm going to do" is evil because it means God is not part of your life. It means thoughts of him do not occur in your head. Your mind is a solid block—of what you expect to do, as if there is no God. To plan with the attitude, "This is what I'm going to do," is evil because you are a practical atheist, living as though God does not exist.

We ought not to plan with any sense of finality or certainty. It's arrogant because we don't know what will happen tomorrow, or even whether we'll be here tomorrow. And it's evil because we're pretending that God does not exist.

And that brings James to the wonderful way we should plan. The only honest, realistic way to plan. "Instead, you ought to say, 'If it is the Lord's will, we will live and do this or that'" (4:15). All our planning, he says, should be with the thought, "Here's what I plan, Lord, assuming it's what you have in mind."

"If it is the Lord's will, we will live"—we'll be around for tomorrow, we'll be here for the future. And, if it is the Lord's will, we will not only live, we'll also "do this or that." "If it is the Lord's will. . ." "Assuming this is what you have in mind, Lord, I'll proceed with the assumption that I'm going to live a bit longer and that this is what you want me to do."

By all means, make your plans. Make your plans to buy a home, switch jobs, pick a college, ask her for a date, reduce your overhead by twenty percent, sell your stocks, land a big account. Make your plans. But make them with the mindset of "If it is the Lord's will." Plan with the conscious thought, "It's really up to God. He controls what happens. Ultimately he's the one who decides." Again and again the Bible says, "We plan, but he decides":

> *In their hearts humans plan their course,*
> *but the LORD establishes their steps.* (Prov. 16:9)

> *Many are the plans in a person's heart,*
> *but it is the LORD's purpose that prevails.* (Prov.19:21)

> *To humans belong the plans of the heart,*
> *but from the LORD comes the proper answer of the tongue.*
> (Prov. 16:1)

We can plan, but the Lord will tell us how it will actually be. In our planning, therefore, we ought to say, "If it is the Lord's will, we will live and do this or that. Here are my plans, Lord, if this is what you have in mind." This is the good way we ought to plan, so let us do it (4:17).

What effect will this good thought have on our lives? What wonderful benefit will we get if we plan this way? It will keep us constantly aware of God's presence and goodness in our lives. If something we planned doesn't happen, we don't need to be disappointed. It means God has something better in mind for us. If something goes differently than what we expected, there's no sense of disaster or catastrophe, only the thought that this is what a good and loving God willed instead. If we live with the thought, "Lord, here's what I'm planning, if it's what you have in mind," we will have the peace of living under his tender care.

What event are you planning in the next month or so? What are you planning this next year that's pretty important to you? If I opened your Day-Timer, if I punched into your phone, if I looked at the calendar hanging on the kitchen wall, what would I see marked down, planned on, circled in red so that nothing else will happen on that date? What would I see? A move? A wedding? A trip? A new job? Look at that date, and say, "Lord, here's what I'm planning, if it's what you have in mind. You can change it if you want to. That's OK. Your way is always good."

A few years ago there were some American Express card commercials featuring the actor Karl Malden. Each commercial would show somebody setting out on a trip—vacationing, shopping, commuting—and something unexpected would happen to them. They would run out of money. Or their wallet would be lost or stolen. Something they didn't anticipate. And at the end of each commercial, Karl Malden would hold up an American Express card and say, "Don't leave home without it."

In a way, James is saying the same thing. Don't leave home, don't set out, don't go into the future, without it—without the thought, "If it is the Lord's will, if it's what you have in mind."

Make your plans in pencil, and know that God has the eraser. And he also has a pen, to write what he wants in ink.

12

MONEY TALKS

James 5:1–6

In the Scripture we're going to look at, James seems at first glance to be talking to a different crowd. He seems to be addressing an audience of wealthy, oppressive sinners. "You rich people," he says, "weep and wail because of the misery that's coming on you! You have done this, and you have done this, and this. And because you have done these things, weep and howl for the misery that's coming to you." We're not sure what to make of this sudden shift in his letter—from an intimate encouragement to believers going through trials, to a prophetic denunciation of rich oppressors.

We're glad of course, that James is not talking to us. We're obviously not rich. "Rich" is a middle-six-figure income, or seven figures, right? And most of us aren't there. So we're relieved that James isn't talking to us. But at the same time we're wondering, as would his original readers, "James, why do you want us to hear what you're saying to someone else? Especially when they're not paying attention to you. The rich aren't listening to you. They aren't going to read your letter. Why do we need to hear what you're saying to them?"

And James's answer to us and his former church members would be: "There are two reasons why I want you to hear what I have to say. First, I want you to hear how God is going to punish the rich for what they've done to you. I want you to know your God is just and fair. When somebody who has more money than you uses it to cheat you, or take something away from you; when they ruin the company you work for, yet get a golden parachute for themselves; when they wipe out your savings or your job while they're still living high; when they use their money to influence the legislature, to twist the system to go their way; when they buy the high-priced lawyers to bury you in the courts; when they use their money to keep you under—I want you to hear what God is going to do to them, the punishment they're going to get. I want you to know that your God is just and fair.

"But there's also a second reason why I want you to hear what I say to them. I want you to hear their sins, so that you will guard your own hearts from them. I want you to hear what God is against, so that in your own life, you will move in the opposite direction. You haven't done the extreme things they've done. But some of you are thinking that by becoming rich you can insulate yourselves from the difficulties of life. You're planning how you can make money (4:13) as a means of protecting yourselves from the trials that come your way. And the great danger is that if you continue with this attitude, you too will fall into the sins of the rich, and the same misery will come on you."

James wants his former church members to persevere through trials to the reward God has for them. To do so, they must not lash out in frustration against each other, but should submit to God's good purposes in the trial. They must also not think that getting wealthy will protect them against the trials. On the contrary, the desire for wealth will make them vulnerable to the very sins of the rich he will mention.

James's warning is doubly valuable for us, for we have already achieved the wealth that many of his readers could only dream about. The average middle class family in America, in terms of their energy consumption— electricity, gas, oil—is benefitting from the equivalent of two hundred personal servants in James's day. Two hundred servants—servants who would wash your clothes, cook your food, light your candles, boil your bathwater, or cool you with fans. Servants who would pull you in a carriage, or who, instead of you using an iPod and an earplug, could provide you with music any time during the day. Servants who at night would perform dramas and comedies for you, just like a TV does today.

In James's day, it took two hundred servants to get what you and I get with the twist of a knob or the flip of a switch or the push of a button. Bill Gates, the Microsoft billionaire, once said, "I'd rather go into any grocery store today than to a king's banquet a hundred years ago. No king ever had what I can get in a grocery store today." No matter how rich the people were in James's day, they couldn't turn a handle for running tap water. They couldn't buy eyeglasses to help them see better. They couldn't take penicillin for dangerous infections. They couldn't put stents in their arteries to help them live longer. And so, when James writes of the dangers of being rich, we want to listen carefully, for we are well into that category, and we need to be cautious lest a further pursuit of wealth become our spiritual undoing.

In the verses we're going to look at, James will identify four sins, four crimes of the rich for which judgment is coming on them.

The first crime, James says, is that the rich accumulate and keep more wealth than they will ever need. And because of this hoarding, misery is coming.

> Now listen, you rich people, weep and wail because of the misery that is coming on you. Your wealth has rotted, and moths have eaten your clothes. Your gold and silver are corroded. Their corrosion will testify against you and eat your flesh like fire. You have hoarded wealth in the last days. (5:1–3)

James refers to the three types of wealth available in his day—food, clothes, and metals. In verse 2 he mentions food—agricultural products, barns full of wheat and barley, baskets of figs, kegs full of wine—agricultural wealth that could rot. Then he mentions a second kind of wealth—clothes, garments, silks, fabrics, chiffons, wools, furs—things that could become moth-eaten. In verse 3 he looks at a third kind—metals that could become tarnished, or that could pick up some acid that would corrode them, or that could simply erode due to constant wear and usage, like when the gold band of a wedding ring gets smaller and smaller due to constant wear and friction. These were the treasures of his day—food, clothes, metals—the wealth that the rich were accumulating and keeping for themselves.

Their crime is that they have hoarded this wealth. They've stored up more than they will ever use. It's just sitting there, like some big fat bank account. No one is using it. No one is getting any benefit from it. James is speaking to those who devote their entire energy to getting and holding as much wealth as possible. Their great satisfaction in life is to see their bank balances get bigger, their investment portfolios expand, their IRAs grow—to watch their net worth get larger and larger. Their answer to the question, "How much is enough?" is the same answer Rockefeller gave: "Just a little bit more."

But now, James says, it's the last days. Human history could end at any moment. God has his hand on the curtain of human history, ready to pull the rope and bring the curtain crashing to the floor. "Show's over, folks." And the ongoing years stop, forever. And there you stand on the stage of life—arms filled with suits, clothes, and furs from your closet, pockets stuffed with gold and jewels, hands clutching bank passbooks, stock certificates, and IRA accounts. But the clothes are starting to disintegrate and smell. The gold Rolex watch no longer runs. The paper in your hand is worthless. And now, in the last days, your useless, rotting, stinking wealth will testify against you.

Money talks, as the saying goes. Your money talks to God. It testifies against you—that you did nothing good with your wealth. You helped no one with it. You kept it all for yourself. There was no raw human need that you alleviated with a large anonymous check. There was no overseas missionary doing God's work whom you supported on a monthly basis. There was no church or Christian organization that you contributed to in a substantial way. No, it was all for yourself. You hoarded it for yourself.

And now, like some flesh-eating bacteria, your riches will eat into your flesh and consume it.

> *Weep and wail because of the misery that is coming on you. Your wealth has rotted, and moths have eaten your clothes. Your gold and silver are corroded. Their corrosion will testify against you and eat your flesh like fire. You have hoarded wealth in the last days.* (5:1–3)

We hear James say these things, and we flinch. We're glad he's not talking to us. But there's something about what he says that makes us a little uncomfortable. Something strikes a little close to home, and a small voice inside us says, "Is that me? Do I do that? Am I like that?" And that small voice bothers us a bit.

Is our net worth growing? Probably so. The value of our home is increasing; our equity is rising. We've probably also done our best to invest wisely. We've tried to make good choices with our IRAs. We intend to combine them with our pensions, savings, and Social Security—and hope we've accumulated enough for a reasonable lifestyle when we retire.

Is our net worth is growing? Yes. Are we accumulating and hanging on to wealth? Yes. But is it more than we will ever need? Are we amassing and hoarding more than we will ever use?

That's not an easy question to answer. It's not all black or white. There are a lot of factors involved. We'll probably use some of our accumulated wealth to help the kids with college. We might also help them buy a home or start a business. We know we'll use some of our wealth for our retirement—but we don't know how much of it we'll need, what with inflation, rising medical costs, expensive surgeries, and long-term health care. And then we'd like to leave some as an inheritance, as a gift to the kids down the line. Even the Bible talks approvingly about leaving an inheritance (2 Cor. 12:14).

Do we have more than we'll ever use? Are we accumulating and keeping, hoarding more than we'll ever need? Or are we being wise, like the ant—laying aside for an unknown future? It's not an easy question to answer.

How could we test ourselves? What's the difference between being prudent and hoarding? When does "preparing for the future" become "accumulating more than I will ever need"? How can we guard ourselves from moving in the direction James is talking about? Let me suggest a very practical way.

Are you giving generously to the Lord? Are you consciously and intentionally, on a regular basis, giving large amounts to the work of God? I don't want to use the word *tithe* because it's misleading. In biblical times people actually gave three tithes, on different amounts.* The total came to about twenty-two percent. So without using the word *tithe*—are you giving generously to the Lord? Somewhere between five percent and fifteen percent?

---

* The first tithe was the worship tithe which supported the work of the temple (Deut. 12:5–6; Mal. 3:10). After this initial 10 percent was subtracted, a second tithe (now 9 percent of the original amount) was used to celebrate God's goodness (Deut. 14:22–27). A third one was the welfare tithe, given every three years,—an additional 2.7 percent tithe on a per annum basis of the remaining 81 percent of the original (Deut. 14:28–29).

If you are, you can be confident that you're guarding your heart. If you're giving away that much, you're not selfishly hoarding for yourself. If you're giving between five percent and fifteen percent of your income, you are sufficiently slowing down and retarding the growth of your bank balance. You are clearly saying that something else is more important than how large your net worth can be.

So, James cautions us first of all to guard against our hoarding wealth, accumulating and keeping it only for ourselves.

The second crime of the rich, James says, is that they make their money at the expense of others—taking advantage of them, cheating them, defrauding them. "There's money in your bank account," he says, "that ought not to be there, because it rightfully belongs to someone else."

> Look! The wages you failed to pay the workers who mowed your fields
> are crying out against you. The cries of the harvesters have reached the
> ears of the Lord Almighty. (5:4)

James is referring to the practice of hiring day laborers for a short-term job. The same thing occurs today as men stand in parking lots or on corners, waiting for a pickup truck to come by and hire them for the day. These men don't have a regular income. They don't have a weekly paycheck. Instead they're dependent on daily work and daily pay. The Old Testament was clear—when you hire a day laborer, you pay him at the end of the day, because he's counting on that pay to buy food for his family that evening:

> Do not take advantage of a hired worker who is poor and needy,
> whether that worker is a fellow Israelite or a foreigner residing in one of
> your towns. Pay them their wages each day before sunset, because they
> are poor and are counting on it. Otherwise they may cry to the LORD
> against you, and you will be guilty of sin. (Deut. 24:14–15)

They will cry to the LORD—an anguished, painful cry. The rich landowner is keeping the money, and there's nothing the poor man can do about it but cry to the Lord.

The poor man cries out. But so does the money of the rich man. Money talks, and the rich man's withheld wages also cry out to the Lord:

The wages you failed to pay the workers who mowed your fields are crying out against you. The cries of the harvesters have reached the ears of the Lord Almighty. (5:4)

The cries of the man and the cries of the money reach the ears of the Lord Almighty. The word *Almighty* is the Hebrew word for "hosts, armies." The cries have reached the ears of the Lord Almighty—the Lord of Hosts, the Lord of Heaven's Armies, the almighty Lord who beckons and commands the destroying forces of heaven, the God of overwhelming power who will avenge the crime. When the cries reach his ears, James says, weep and howl for the misery that will come on you. We hear the anger of our God against such dishonesty—making money at the expense of others—and we want to move in the opposite direction. How can we guard our hearts?

We guard our hearts by making sure there's nothing in our bank account that belongs to someone else—no money we've gained and kept at the expense of others. No churning of investment portfolios just for the commissions without adding to value to the investor. No unnecessary phone calls or useless paperwork just to create "billable hours." No one that we've fired in their fifties just so we can hire someone younger at a lower salary and lower health costs. No one that we've let go just before their pension became vested or qualified, so that we don't have to pay out benefits. No prescribing unnecessary medical tests just because we get a percentage of the lab income. No longstanding unpaid bills to mechanics or doctors. No personal loans from friends that we've delayed paying back. No selling of generators at three times their value when hurricanes or floods have knocked out electric power. No personal bankruptcies that left our creditors holding the bag and that we're not trying to make good on. We guard our hearts by knowing that there's nothing in our bank account that rightfully belongs to another, no money we've gained or kept at the expense of others.

The third crime of the rich for which judgment will come, James says, is their excessive consumption. Their lifestyle is indulgent and self-centered, their spending has no limits, their luxury has no boundaries.

You have lived on earth in luxury and self-indulgence. You have fattened yourselves in the day of slaughter. (5:5)

It's a picture of self-indulgence without thought of the spiritual effect it may be having on us. Spending on luxuries without regard for spiritual damage: amusements and entertainments that break down boundaries and restraints; cable television at the cost of morals; weekend cabins at the cost of weekly worship; limos for the prom, and hotel rooms afterwards, at the cost of purity. Buying anything and everything. "Last year's computer is too slow. Last year's cell phone only has twenty-seven features instead of fifty-three like this year's. Clothes closets are jam-packed, but new styles have come out, and I gotta have them."

Don't misunderstand. The Bible is not against spending money for the good things of life. In fact, the Old Testament tells God's people that they should do something that would be fairly equivalent to our spending nine percent of our yearly salary on a family vacation (Deut. 14:22–26). The Bible says that God is the giver of every good and perfect gift (James 1:17), and that he richly provides us with everything for our enjoyment (1 Tim. 6:17). The Bible is not against personal expenditures; rather, it encourages us to enjoy the good things God gives us.

What James is talking about, however, is a picture of excessive consumption, indulgent and self-centered spending that has no boundaries and ignores the spiritual consequences. Like cattle fattening themselves in a feedlot, stuffing themselves with anything they want, marbling the fat, gaining more, hour by hour, yet unaware that each day is bringing the butcher closer, "the day of slaughter." An excessive lifestyle, oblivious to the spiritual consequences, unaware of the judgment that is coming.

How do we protect ourselves? How do we guard our hearts? We guard ourselves by saying, "There are some things we won't do as a family, because it wouldn't be good for us. And there are some things we won't buy. Just because we can afford it doesn't mean we will buy it. The car we have is good enough. The clothes we have look fine. We can live without the latest electronic toys. One caramel macchiato a week is enough." We guard our hearts by not always buying more.

James mentions one final crime of the rich: they use their money to bully and destroy others. They use their connections, their networks, their knowledge of the system, their ability to pass out favors and influence, to crush the innocent and powerless:

> *You have condemned and murdered the innocent one, who was not opposing you.* (5:6)

James's readers knew the abuses in their nation's history, and God's promised judgment: Ahab and Jezebel falsely accusing and legally murdering Naboth in order to seize his vineyard for a palace expansion (1 Kings 21); land barons using violence to buy the neighboring houses and vineyards for miles around, until they're the only landowners in the area (Isa. 5:7–8). But God will impoverish their rapacious grabs: ten acres of their vines will produce only one bucket of wine, a wagonload of their seed will produce only one bucket of grain (Isa. 5:9–10).

In our day, violence and injustice at the hands of the rich may be a bit more sophisticated, but it still occurs. Through judicial bribes, witness tampering, and high-priced lawyers, they destroy those who are hoping for justice. Through price-fixing and the capacity to absorb a temporary loss, they put a small competitor out of business. Through cronyism and kickbacks, they get the city to declare eminent domain on a coveted parcel of land, and then develop it to the benefit of their coffers and the city's tax base, leaving the poor without homes to live in. Through turning apartments into condos, they evict elderly tenants and sell the units for large sums, thumbing their noses at rent controls designed to protect the vulnerable.

Perhaps it comes even closer to home—if we ever prevent someone from moving into our neighborhood lest our property values suffer, or if we ever stand by silently, protecting our own jobs and finances, while our Christian organization throws an innocent worker to the wolves to satisfy a wealthy contributor. The spirit of Caiaphas seeps in so easily: "Better that one should suffer than that we all pay a price" (John 11:49-50).

It's understandable that all of us want a reasonable degree of wealth. Money can protect us from a host of ills, just as it could protect James's readers from the trials they were going through. But some of these ills and trials are of God's design, intended to make us "mature and complete, not lacking anything" (1:3). And our primary goal is not necessarily to avoid them, but rather to persevere through them to the reward God has promised.

To persevere, we must guard ourselves from the all-too-common sins of the rich, lest misery come upon us. We know we are guarding ourselves when we give generously to the Lord, when we have no money that belongs to another, when we are circumspect in our purchases and activities, and when we are willing to risk our own economics for the sake of justice to another.

As we do these things, the crown of life settles upon us (1:12).

13

THE MOMENT OF THE LORD'S MERCY

James 5:7–12

James has something very loving to say to his suffering friends, and to us. And it's this: Hang in there, mercy is coming. Hang in there, keep going, stay with it, mercy is coming. If you're living with disappointment, if you're living with loneliness, if you're living with tears, hang in there, mercy is coming. If you've been treated unfairly, if you've been rejected, if you've been forced into a life or circumstances you never intended, hang in there, mercy is coming. If you're burdened with illness, or with aging parents, if you have a rough marriage or rebellious children, hang in there, keep going, persevere. Mercy is coming.

The Lord will return, and when he does, he will be full of mercy. There's a time when he'll come back, and when he does, he'll make everything up to you. He'll turn your disappointment and rejection into honor and praise. He'll turn your illness into vibrant health. He'll turn your loneliness into unending friendship and laughter. He'll remove all the hardships and difficulties. And he'll bring every joy or fullness that you've longed for.

Hang in there, the Lord is coming, and when he does, he will turn every sorrow into joy:

> Be patient, then, brothers and sisters, until the Lord's coming. See how the farmer waits for the land to yield its valuable crop, patiently waiting for the autumn and spring rains. You too, be patient and stand firm, because the Lord's coming is near. Don't grumble against one

another, brothers and sisters, or you will be judged. The Judge is standing at the door!

Brothers and sisters, as an example of patience in the face of suffering, take the prophets who spoke in the name of the Lord. As you know, we count as blessed those who have persevered. You have heard of Job's perseverance and have seen what the Lord finally brought about. The Lord is full of compassion and mercy.

Above all, my brothers and sisters, do not swear—not by heaven or by earth or by anything else. All you need to say is a simple "Yes" or "No." Otherwise you will be condemned. (5:7–12)*

"Hang in there," James says in verse 8—"be patient and stand firm, because the Lord's coming is near." We're all waiting for him expectantly, and his arrival could occur at any moment. It's as though he's coming up the front walkway, and any moment he'll come through the door and be here. And when he comes, you'll receive all of his mercy and compassion. So hang in there; his arrival could be any second, and when it happens, all of life will be changed to what it should be.

Be like the farmer, James says in verse 7: "See how the farmer waits." He waits patiently; he hangs in there through the tough days. He's waiting for the reward he knows is coming—he waits for the land to yield its valuable crop."

James is picturing a small-farm owner. The farmer has carefully saved some seed and planted it in the ground. And now all of his attention is centered on the valuable crop that will come. And he waits. He waits patiently through the early autumn rains which saturate the soil so that the new seed can germinate. He waits patiently through the late spring rains which give

---

* James 5:7–12 is written in an *a-b-a-b* pattern. The *a*'s are James's encouragement to wait patiently, and the *b*'s are our ways of showing that we are doing it. This structure becomes apparent if we combine the common elements:

Wait patiently:

a Hang in there through suffering, for mercy is coming (5:7–8).

a The Lord will return and all of life will be made right (5:10–11).

Show your patience by:

b Not grumbling against other believers (5:9).

b Not compromising your integrity in order to lessen your pressures (5:12).

the surge of growth to the emerging plant. He waits through the final weeks, maybe living on short rations, skimping on meals, hanging in there to the moment when the valuable crop comes as his reward.

Hang in there, my friend, for when Christ arrives, he brings the reward with him. There is mercy coming.

James goes on to say there are two ways you can tell if someone is waiting patiently, two ways to tell if someone is hanging in there, genuinely trusting the Lord, waiting for him to bring the reward. The first way is that the person doesn't complain about the fact that other Christians may have it better than he does and doesn't resent what God has chosen to do for others; there is not grumbling about others having better circumstances.

Don't grumble against each other, brothers and sisters, or you will be judged. The Judge is standing at the door! (5:9)

Those who wait patiently, trusting that God's goodness will come, don't resent what God has done for someone else. They don't complain that someone else has a higher income, or better health, or a marriage and family. They don't grumble that someone else got the raise or promotion they wanted, or got into the school they were applying for. Someone who is waiting and looking for the Lord's reward doesn't complain to God, "How come they have it, and I don't?" To grumble and complain is to say to God, "You're not fair. You're the Judge, and you're not fair. You haven't been good to me."

And the Judge, the Judge who's come up the walkway and is standing at the door—the Judge who has his hand on the doorknob, ready to enter the room with his full reward—the Judge outside the door will hear that complaint, and when he comes into the room, there will be disappointment in his eyes and a frown on his face, for here he was, ready to give his full reward.

The first sign, James says, of those who are waiting patiently for the goodness the Lord is bringing is that they don't resent what God may have given another, for they know the Lord is going to be good to them also, and that a moment is coming when all of God's compassion and mercy will be poured on them.

The second sign, the second way you know those who are waiting and trusting patiently, James says, is that they don't compromise their integrity or honesty in order to make things easier on themselves. They don't falsify or distort; they don't misrepresent or fabricate. They're truthful and open—on insurance forms and school applications, on financial statements, and in business arrangements. They're honest and forthright—about their dating history or their health issues, about their work experience or their financial assets. They don't maneuver or finesse or shade the truth in any way in order to ease the difficulties.

> *Above all, my brothers and sisters, do not swear—not by heaven or by earth or by anything else. All you need to say is a simple "Yes" or "No." Otherwise, you will be condemned.* (5:12)

James is looking at a situation where someone, under pressure or stress to avoid some hardship, might insist that something is true, even though it isn't. In order to deceive and convince the other person, so as to make things easier for himself, someone may even take an oath—"I swear it!"—and insist on something more than necessary—"I really mean it, I promise, cross my heart, God is my witness"—trying to convince the other person in order to get himself out of a difficulty. But someone who is waiting patiently, someone who knows that the Lord's goodness is coming, will never compromise his integrity or honesty in order to make things easier on himself. Instead, you can trust what he says absolutely. When he says something is so, it's so—his "Yes" is a truthful yes, his "No" is a truthful no.

These are the two signs of people who are trusting God and waiting for his mercy—they don't complain about their treatment, and they don't compromise the truth. Because they know that when the Lord comes into the room, God's full mercy and compassion will be poured on them.

And then, to conclude his encouragement for us to hang in there, to wait patiently, James asks us to look at the examples of others who persevered through hardship and found that the Lord was indeed full of compassion and mercy:

> *Brothers and sisters, as an example of patience in the face of suffering, take the prophets who spoke in the name of the Lord. As you know, we count as blessed those who have persevered. You have heard of Job's*

perseverance and have seen what the Lord finally brought about. The Lord is full of compassion and mercy. (5:10–11)

Consider the prophets, he says. They did what God asked them to do—they spoke in the name of the Lord. But speaking the Lord's word, confronting their societies, often brought hardship and suffering to the ones doing the speaking. But they were patient in the face of suffering, they persevered.

Take the prophet Jeremiah. Jeremiah was arrested because of his public statements—because of the word of the Lord that he gave his contemporaries. When Jeremiah's trial came, people he had known all his life lied and testified against him. They committed perjury in order to spare themselves. Even before the trial began, the judge had already written out the verdict—guilty. And when the charade was over, when the kangaroo court had ended, Jeremiah found himself in a mucky pit. But he was patient in the face of suffering.

Take the prophet Ezekiel. Ezekiel spoke the words God gave him to guide his people during their Babylonian captivity. But at every turn, older leaders among the people, men with more influence than Ezekiel, contradicted him and humiliated him publicly. And while all this was going on, his young wife died. The wife who believed in him, who brought him what little joy he had on earth, was gone. And Ezekiel was alone in his pain and rejection. But still he kept on. He hung in there.

Take the prophet Daniel. One day as a child Daniel saw foreign soldiers smash down the door to his house. They came in, grabbed him roughly by the arm, and hauled him away from his family. They were speaking a language he didn't understand, and they were taking him and other boys his age off to a foreign country, never to see their families again. He was forced to grow up in that strange culture. He was given a new, strange-sounding name—Belteshazzar. He had to learn the foreign language, for they were educating him to serve the nation that had captured him.

These are the prophets who spoke in the name of the Lord and who persevered patiently through suffering. And yet when we think about them, we don't think about these things. These trials aren't the things that we remember about them.

Instead, we think of how they were blessed, how uniquely favored they were. "As you know," James says, we count them as blessed, because we're more impressed with how God's goodness showed in their lives than the trials they went through. We don't think of their sufferings, we think instead of what God revealed to them. We think instead of the wonderful truths God gave them, truths they passed on to us.

Take Jeremiah again. Jeremiah is the one who told us that we weren't going to have to be under the old covenant of the law any more, a covenant which always made us feel condemned for our failure to keep it. Instead, he wrote, God was going to make a new covenant with us. God was going to put his own Spirit within us, a Spirit that would enable us to live in ways pleasing to him.

Or take Ezekiel. Ezekiel revealed to us God's plans to someday build a new temple, a temple which would be filled with the brilliance and majesty of his Son.

And Daniel. Daniel gave us the timetable that told us when that Son would actually come to earth and walk among us as our Savior.

> Brothers and sisters, as an example of patience in the face of suffering, take the prophets who spoke in the name of the Lord. As you know, we count as blessed those who have persevered. (5:10–11a)

Hang in there. The Lord's goodness and mercy are coming.

And then finally, James says, take Job. Recall his experience, and you'll see what God is like. You'll see what God is ultimately going to do for you. You'll see how he's just waiting for the moment when he can let his compassion and mercy flood over you. Take Job:

> You have heard of Job's perseverance and have seen what the Lord finally brought about. The Lord is full of compassion and mercy. (5:11b)

You've heard of Job. He was a godly man. A man of wealth. A man honored by his contemporaries. A man who raised a large family, and his children enjoyed being with each other. As they grew into adulthood, they looked forward to family gatherings and took pleasure in each other's company. And Job was grateful for all of God's goodness to him.

But one day, unknown to Job, Satan began to challenge God about Job. Satan claimed the only reason Job worshipped God was because God had given him a good life. "Take away the good life you've given him," Satan said, "let some suffering come his way, and he'll stop serving you. In fact, he'll curse you, and turn away from you."

God accepted the challenge, because he knew Satan's accusation wasn't true. He knew that Job loved him for who he was, and not for what he had given him. So God gave Satan permission to undo Job's circumstances. "You'll find out, Satan, that he serves me for who I am, and not for the life I've given him."

And so, in one afternoon, Satan was allowed to change Job's life from wealth and joy to poverty and sorrow. In the space of a few hours, Job's entire net worth and family were lost. Every asset he had, every source of income, was stripped from him. Raiders stole his herds and killed his hired hands. A tornado claimed the lives of all his children. Job was in shock. Stunned, he fell on his face before the Lord. He lay there, trying to find God, wanting to know why such overwhelming sorrow should descend on him. No understanding came to him. But when he rose, his answer to others was, "The Lord gave it, and the Lord took it away. And I will continue to look to the Lord." He hung in there.

Satan was infuriated by Job's trust. "I'm not finished," he said to God. "Let me do more. Let me touch his body, let me affect him physically." Satan accused God of leaving Job with enough physical and mental resources to stay strong in the suffering. "Yeah, yeah, sure, as long as he feels good mentally and physically, he can hang in there. But let me add pain and suffering to his sorrow and poverty, and then let's see how long he lasts. He'll curse you for sure." And so God gave Satan permission to affect Job physically.

And Satan hit Job with an infectious disease that blistered his whole body, from his head to his feet. All day long his pain was unbelievable. Yet when his wife asked why he still worshipped God, Job's answer was, "Do we give God the right to only send us good things, but never to allow us trouble?" And to his friends he said, "Though he slay me, yet will I trust him."

More than once Job asked God, "Why?" More than once, in a moment of frustration, he insisted that he hadn't done anything to deserve what happened to him. He asked God for a reason. At one point, overwhelmed by the magnitude and unendingness of his trouble, he said to God, "I want to know why my life is like this." And he demanded that God give him an explanation.

At which point God said, "Job, do you have a right to demand anything from me? Do I owe you an explanation of how I run my universe? When I created the earth, Job, where were you? I don't recall your being back there with me, helping me do it. When I timed the earth's daily rotation, and planned its orbit through the sky, I don't remember your contribution to that either. Over the centuries, I've made billions of snowflakes, no two of them alike—billions, and not a duplicate among them. It seems to me, Job, that I'm pretty much in control of what's going on in my universe. Am I accountable to you for it? Do I owe you an explanation, or do I—as the one who created you and brought you into existence, the one who even gives you the next breath you're going to take—do I have the right arrange your life as I want? Do I, Job?"

And Job bowed. "Of course you do. You have the right to do as you want. You owe me no explanation." And God said, "That's what I wanted to hear." And that was the end of the conversation.

Job never did get an explanation. For the rest of his life, he never learned the reason why those things happened to him—that God was proving to Satan that a man would continue to trust him, not knowing what God was doing, but simply believing that God would be ultimately good.

And God was good. Mercy did come. James says in verse 11—

You have heard of Job's perseverance and have seen what the Lord finally brought about. The Lord is full of compassion and mercy.

The Lord restored Job's financial worth, and even doubled it. And Job found himself with even greater influence and honor in his community. Other children were born who were even more of a delight to him. His daughters were known throughout the country for their beauty. And he lived to see his great-great-grandchildren. But he never learned why he went through a period of such intense trouble and sorrow.

My friend, you too may never know the reason for your trouble. It may have nothing to do with you; it may have nothing to do with anyone around you. It may simply be that God is again showing the Evil One that you love him—not for his gifts, nor for his blessings—but for himself, for who he is, for the salvation he's given you, for the privilege of knowing him for eternity.

And God asks you to trust him, to wait patiently, to believe that there's a moment coming when his overwhelming compassion and mercy will flood you, and all of life will be made right.

Hang in there. Mercy is coming.

14

THE PRAYER OF FAITH

James 5:13–20

In the final paragraphs of his letter, James writes some sentences that have raised no end of questions among Christians:

Is anyone among you sick? Let them call the elders of the church to pray over them and anoint them with oil in the name of the Lord. And the prayer offered in faith will make the sick person well; the Lord will raise them up. (5:14–15a)

Are we supposed to do this whenever we're sick—call for the elders to pray over us? Is this a guarantee of healing—they'll pray and we'll get well? If so, something isn't working! As we try to understand these sentences, let's fit them into James's overall flow of thought through his closing paragraphs.

James's theme in 5:13–20 is, "Whatever is going on in your life, or in the lives of those you care about, you should be talking to God about it. Whatever is happening to you or to others, you should be praying about it." He'll stress this theme four times, bringing up four situations, four events of life, as examples of things we ought to be praying about. And within this overall flow, we'll find his sentences about the prayer offered in faith. Let's look at the four examples he mentions.

First, James says, we ought to pray whenever we are in trouble:

Is anyone among you in trouble? Let them pray. (5:13a)

We ought to pray when things go wrong—when we're frustrated at work, when we don't have enough money to pay our bills, when a friendship is turning sour, when there's a difficulty in our family, when our child doesn't have any friends at school, when trials are hitting us, when bad things are happening. Instead of complaining, grumbling, getting bitter, or lashing out at others, we should pray about it. We should believe that God is in the situation and is using it in some way to make us like his Son. Ask him what his purposes are, pray for insight, pray for direction as to how to act. Ask him to use his power to change the circumstances so that great praise can be given to him. Whenever you are in trouble, pray.

Second, we ought to pray whenever we are happy:

Is anyone happy? Let them sing songs of praise. (5:13b)

We ought to pray when things are going good—we got a raise or a promotion, we made the last payment on our car, we got the schedule at school that we wanted, the family with the barking dog moved away, our child made a new friend, our dental exam revealed no cavities. Whenever we are buoyant and in good spirits, we ought to give thanks to God, singing psalms of praise, our joy ascending like a melody:

Thy Loving Kindness is Better Than Life (Ps. 63)

I Will Sing of the Mercies of the Lord Forever (Ps. 89)

O Lord, Our Lord, How Majestic Is Your Name (Ps. 8)

When we are happy, we want to acknowledge that every good and perfect gift is from above (1:17) and give thanks to God.

James's first two examples have to do with ourselves—our lives, our situations. His third and fourth examples have to do with others—the circumstances of people we care about, friends at church, fellow believers. We should be praying for them, he says, when we see that they are either seriously ill (vv. 14–15) or struggling with sin (vv. 16a, 19–20). The reason we ought to pray in these situations is because:

The prayer of a righteous person is powerful and effective. (5:16b)

A righteous person is not someone who is sinlessly perfect, but someone who is simply walking with God, caring about what God wants, wanting to honor and obey him. A righteous person is an ordinary, normal person who wants to serve God. A person like Elijah:

Elijah was a human being, even as we are. He prayed earnestly that it would not rain, and it did not rain on the land for three and a half years. Again he prayed, and the heavens gave rain, and the earth produced its crops. (5:17–18)

Elijah was an ordinary person, just like us. He had the same emotions, weaknesses, vulnerabilities, and strengths we have. He had his moments of intense commitment and overwhelming trust—he could call down fire from heaven (1 Kings 18). But he also sometimes sank into the depths of despair and depression, telling God that he'd had enough and wanted out (1 Kings 19). One day he could be brave and determined in front of the king, but the next day he fled the country in fear of the queen. Yet, he was a righteous person—he cared about God's honor and God's people. And the prayers of this ordinary human being were powerful and effective.

Your prayers are powerful and effective. Be encouraged by the Scriptures which tell you that God listens to you when your heart is clean and your desire is to obey:

Who may ascend the mountain of the Lord?
Who may stand in his holy place?
The one who has clean hands and a pure heart. (Ps. 24:3–4a)

If I had cherished sin in my heart,
The Lord would not have listened;
But God has surely listened
and has heard my prayer. (Ps. 66:18–19)

Dear friends, if our hearts do not condemn us, we have confidence before God and receive from him anything we ask, because we keep his commands and do what pleases him. (1 John 3:21–22)

Since our prayers will be powerfully effective, James says, thirdly, that we ought to pray for those who are seriously ill:

Is anyone among you sick? Let them call the elders of the church to pray over them and anoint them with oil in the name of the Lord. And the prayer offered in faith will make the sick person well; the Lord will raise them up. If they have sinned, they will be forgiven. (5:14–15)

Since these sentences have caused so much confusion among Christians, let's look carefully at what James is saying.

First, he's looking at situations where the person is seriously sick. This is not a twenty-four hour flu, nor a minor operation, nor the end-of-life demise, nor even a heart attack from which the individual is recovering. Instead, the sickness in view is a long-term debilitation that has progressively incapacitated the individual. Though our English translation uses the same word *sick* in both verses 14 and 15, James, in his language, actually uses two different words. In verse 14, he uses a word that means "weak." But in verse 15, he uses a stronger word that means "weary, worn down, exhausted." James is talking about a situation where a bed-ridden individual has gotten weaker and weaker over a prolonged period of time, to the point where going to the elders is no longer an option; instead, the ill person calls for the elders to come to him.

Second, the individual's sickness may be because they have sinned. Not all sickness, of course, is due to sin. But some is: abuses of the Lord's Supper (1 Cor. 11:29–30) and persistent refusal to respond to God's discipline (1 John 5:16–17) can result in physical deterioration and even death. The elders would gently probe this area with the individual, who may or may not see a connection between some past sin and his present weakened condition. If the elders are able to lead the individual to repentance, then forgiveness can occur, and healing can become possible.

Third, while such individuals may have sought the prayers of many believers, they are specifically encouraged to "call the elders of the church to pray over them and anoint them with oil in the name of the Lord."

The elders are the leaders of the congregation, responsible for the spiritual care of the congregation. Though they are ordinary human beings, they are also righteous men who will discern how God wants them to pray in the situation (more on this in a moment). The elders will "anoint them with oil in the name of the Lord." This oil is not medicinal. Presumably the individual would long since have sought whatever medical help might be available. And while it's possible the oil might have some medicinal value for open sores, it would have no effect on broken bones or internal diseases and injuries. Instead, the oil is a sign that righteous men have gathered in the name of the Lord to discern how to pray for this seriously sick person. The oil is a sign that the elders are focusing on the Lord's presence in the situation and seeking his leading. For while they have no question about God's power to heal, they must first determine whether he intends to or not.

This brings us finally to "the prayer offered in faith" which will make the sick well and cause the Lord to raise them up. What is this "prayer offered in faith"?

This is not the prayer that sometimes occurs when believers have been urged fervently to "have faith, and just believe God for it." That kind of prayer is nothing more than believers convincing themselves that what they want is what God is going to do, and that if they can pray loud enough and long enough, they can convince God to do it. This is not a prayer of faith at all, but only a "psyching of ourselves" into thinking that our conviction will determine God's action. Such a prayer will always fail and lead to disappointment.

The prayer offered in faith is a prayer that believes something *God has already said* and prays in line with that. Faith is always a response to some *prior* statement or promise from God. Biblical faith is when you *already know* what God's promises or intentions are, and you're willing to act or pray accordingly to bring them about.

Many times in Scripture God's promise or intention is actually given in the past tense—"I have already done such-and-such, so you should believe that it has essentially occurred, and therefore act to make it happen." God's words to Joshua about conquering a city are one such instance:

> Then the LORD said to Joshua, "Do not be afraid; do not be discouraged. Take the whole army with you, and go up and attack Ai. For **I have delivered** into your hands the king of Ai, his people, his city and his

land. You shall do to Ai and its king as you did to Jericho and its king. (Josh. 8:1–2a, emphasis mine)

Joshua then led his troops into battle because he had faith in what God had already said to him. Faith is always a response to some previous statement or promise from God.

James's use of Elijah as an example is very instructive. The prayer of this ordinary human being was a prayer of faith—he *already knew* God's intentions when he declared that it would not rain, and again, when he later prayed for the rain to resume. His prayers were offered in faith—they were obedient, believing responses to something God had already written or told him. Elijah appears abruptly in Ahab's court, declaring, "It's not going to rain until I give the word" (1 Kings 17:1). What made Elijah think he could pull that off? Could you go into the local weather bureau and announce, "No rain until I say so"? What made Elijah think it would happen as he said?

Because he had been reading what God had said to Moses:

> *If you faithfully obey the commands I am giving you today—to love the LORD your God and to serve him with all your heart and with all your soul—then I will send rain on your land in its season, both autumn and spring rains, so that you may gather in your grain, new wine and olive oil. I will provide grass in the fields for your cattle, and you will eat and be satisfied.*
>
> *Be careful, or you will be enticed to turn away and worship other gods and bow down to them. Then the LORD's anger will burn against you, and he will shut up the heavens so that it will not rain and the ground will yield no produce, and you will soon perish from the good land the LORD is giving you.* (Deut. 11:13–17)

> *If you do not obey the LORD your God and do not carefully follow all his commands and decrees I am giving you today, all these curses will come on you and overtake you: . . . The sky over your head will be bronze, the ground beneath you iron. The LORD will turn the rain of your country into dust and powder; it will come down from the skies until you are destroyed.* (Deut. 28:15, 23–24)

God had promised what would happen in the land if the people failed to obey him and went after other gods. And as Elijah witnessed the worst king in Israel's history on the throne, a king who promoted and led apostate worship in the land (1 Kings 16:29–33), he prayed, "Surely, Lord, if there was ever a time when these judgments should fall, now is the time." And the voice of the Spirit said to Elijah, "Yes, Elijah, now, through you. Go tell Ahab that it's not going to rain until you give the word." And in faith Elijah made the announcement to Ahab.

Three years later God spoke to Elijah again, announcing his intention to resume the rain:

> *After a long time, in the third year, the word of the LORD came to Elijah: "Go and present yourself to Ahab, and I will send rain on the land." So Elijah went to present himself to Ahab.* (1 Kings 18:1–2)

As the contest on Carmel unfolds, Elijah already knows that God is going to send rain. And when the contest is over, he begins to pray in faith for the rain to happen. Seven times he prays, with no evidence of any rain coming (1 Kings 18:43–45). But he keeps praying, for he hears the sound of a heavy rain (1 Kings 18:41–42), even though no sound is there. In other words, he is praying confidently, in faith, because he already knows what God intends to do.

That's how the elders should approach a request to come and pray for a sick person. Before they pray for God to heal, they should first determine if that's God's intention. They should spend some time at the bedside, or perhaps even at the church before they caravan to the home of the sick, asking, "God, how do you want us to pray? Should we pray for a healing? Is that what you intend to do? Or is this sickness a trial intended to develop maturity and completeness in the person? If so, should we pray for perseverance and trust, rather than for healing?"

It is not always God's intention to heal. Paul left Trophimus sick in Miletus (2 Tim. 4:20). Paul also learned that his own thorn in the flesh was not going to be removed, since it was enabling Christ's power to rest on him (2 Cor. 12:7–10). Healing was not God's intention in either case.

The elders, therefore, should first discern God's intention. And if they collectively sense that God intends to heal, then they will pray accordingly, and "the prayer offered in faith will make the sick person well; the Lord will raise him up."

I remember when I first came as a young pastor to a church in Arizona. After I'd been there a few months, I got a call one morning in my office from Martha, one of the elderly ladies in the church. "Hi, Martha, what's up?" "Oh, Don, Art [her husband] is in the hospital. He's in terrible pain. He has a kidney stone, and it won't move, and the doctors don't know what to do. They don't want to operate, because he's an old man, but they can't leave him in pain much longer either." "Martha, I'm sorry to hear that. What hospital is he at? I'll stop by this afternoon." "Oh that would be good, Don," and she told me where he was.

As I hung up, before I turned my mind back to what I was doing when the call came in, I briefly prayed, "Lord, how should I minister to Art when I get to the hospital later today? What should I say to him? What should I pray?" And out of the blue, a "voice" spoke in my mind, "Tell Art that you're going to ask me to pass the stone, and that I will do it, and he won't need surgery."

After I silently recovered my breath, I said, "Lord, I don't want to say that. I'm a new, young pastor here; I need all the credibility I can get. If I say that, and you don't do it, I'll look foolish, and they'll wonder about my stability."

"Don, say it! Tell Art that you're going to ask me, and I'm going to pass the stone!" "O-o-okay, Lord. I'll say it."

All afternoon I dreaded the visit at the hospital. When I finally got there and arrived at the room, Martha and Art were sitting in chairs on one side of the room, Art rather uncomfortably. Sitting in another chair across from them, however, was Jim, a friend from church. Jim was an architect with some freedom in his schedule, and he was doing a fine Christian thing—visiting the sick in the hospital. But I didn't need another witness!

For the next half hour I hemmed and hawed in conversation, wondering how I was going to work in the impossible prayer that I thought God wanted me to offer. But after half an hour, before I got the nerve to say anything, Art suddenly informed me, "Don, they've scheduled surgery for 6:30 tomorrow morning. The stone hasn't moved at all, and they can't wait any longer."

"Oh, Art, I'm sorry to hear that. Well, let me pray before I go. 'Lord, guide the hand of the surgeon . . .'" and I proceeded to give that "safe" prayer.

On the way out of the hospital, I was puzzled. "Lord, I thought I was supposed to pray and you were going to pass the stone. But the surgery was already scheduled. I don't understand."

The next morning I was at my desk when the phone rang. It was Martha. "Martha, how's Art?"

"Oh, Don, you'll never guess what happened—last night Art passed the stone." "Ah . . . that's good, Martha, I'm glad to hear that, thanks for letting me know. Good-bye."

As I turned my face upward, I heard the voice: "Sunukjian, you blew it! I gave you a chance to look really good, and you blew it!" "I know. Give me another chance."

There are times when we'll know in advance what God intends to do. And then we can ask according to his will, and he will do it. Regretfully, at that young age, I didn't quite have the faith to follow through.

Finally, James says, we should pray for those who are struggling with sin:

> Therefore confess your sins to each other and pray for each other so that you may be healed. The prayer of a righteous person is powerful and effective. . . . My brothers and sisters, if one of you should wander from the truth and someone should bring that person back, remember this: Whoever turns a sinner from the error of their way will save them from death and cover over a multitude of sins. (5:16,19–20)

James seems to broaden his comments here to include other righteous people, besides elders, praying for fellow believers who are in the initial stages of sin. When we see someone begin to wander from the truth, we should come alongside that person and pray for him or her before the consequences of sin become severe. We should come in humility, knowing that we too are sinners, with our own failures to confess. And as we pray for one another, we turn each other from the error of our way and save each other from death.

Close friends can have this ministry to each other. When we see a friend reacting poorly to a situation, not handling something well, or when we see foolish and irresponsible behavior, or when we see sexual impurity or addiction emerging, we know that our prayers can be powerful and effective. Through this mutual confession, prayer, and healing, we cover over a multitude of sins, removing them from sight and restoring one another to God.

Pray when you are in trouble. Pray when you are happy. Pray for those who are seriously ill. Pray for those who are struggling with sin. And through these prayers, the blessing of James will come upon us:

> *Blessed is the one who perseveres under trial because, having stood the test, that person will receive the crown of life that the Lord has promised to those who love him. (1:12)*